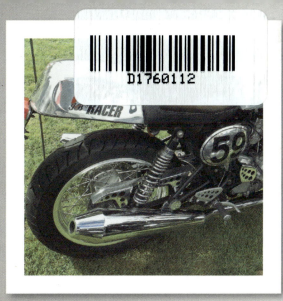

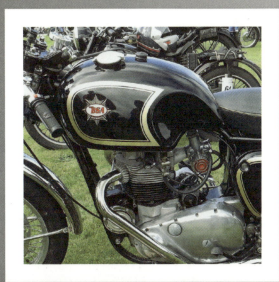

BRITISH
CAFÉ RACERS

Uli Cloesen

Speedpro Series
Harley-Davidson Evolution Engines, How to Build & Power Tune (Hammill)
Motorcycle-engined Racing Car, How to Build (Pashley)

RAC handbooks
Caring for your scooter – How to maintain & service your 49cc to 125cc twist & go scooter (Fry)
How your motorcycle works – Your guide to the components & systems of modern motorcycles (Henshaw)
Motorcycles – A first-time-buyer's guide (Henshaw)

Enthusiast's Restoration Manual Series
Beginner's Guide to Classic Motorcycle Restoration YOUR step-by-step guide to setting up a workshop, choosing a project, dismantling, sourcing parts, renovating & rebuilding classic motorcyles from the 1970s & 1980s, The (Burns)
Classic Large Frame Vespa Scooters, How to Restore (Paxton)
Ducati Bevel Twins 1971 to 1986 (Falloon)
How to restore Honda CX500 & CX650 – YOUR step-by-step colour illustrated guide to complete restoration (Burns)
How to restore Honda Fours – YOUR step-by-step colour illustrated guide to complete restoration (Burns)
Triumph Trident T150/T160 & BSA Rocket III, How to Restore (Rooke)
Yamaha FS1-E, How to Restore (Watts)

Essential Buyer's Guide Series
BMW 'Airhead' Twins (Henshaw)
BMW GS (Henshaw)
BSA 350 & 500 Unit Construction Singles (Henshaw)
BSA 500 & 650 Twins (Henshaw)
BSA Bantam (Henshaw)
Ducati Bevel Twins (Falloon)
Ducati Desmodue Twins (Falloon)
Ducati Desmoquattro Twins – 851, 888, 916, 996, 998, ST4 1988 to 2004 (Falloon)
Harley-Davidson Big Twins (Henshaw)
Hinckley Triumph triples & fours 750, 900, 955, 1000, 1050, 1200 – 1991-2009 (Henshaw)
Honda CBR FireBlade (Henshaw)
Honda CBR600 Hurricane (Henshaw)
Honda SOHC Fours 1969-1984 (Henshaw)
Kawasaki Z1 & Z900 (Orritt)
Moto Guzzi 2-valve big twins (Falloon)
Norton Commando (Henshaw)
Piaggio Scooters - all modern four-stroke automatic models 1991 to 2016 (Willis)
Royal Enfield Bullet (Henshaw)
Triumph 350 & 500 Twins (Henshaw)
Triumph Bonneville (Henshaw)
Triumph Thunderbird, Trophy & Tiger (Henshaw)
Velocette 350 & 500 Singles (Henshaw)
Vespa Scooters – Classic 2-stroke models 1960-2008 (Paxton)

Those Were The Days ... Series
Brighton National Speed Trials (Gardiner)
British Drag Racing – The early years (Pettitt)
Café Racer Phenomenon, The (Walker)
Drag Bike Racing in Britain – From the mid '60s to the mid '80s (Lee)

Biographies
Chris Carter at Large – Stories from a lifetime in motorcycle racing (Carter & Skelton)
Edward Turner – The Man Behind the Motorcycles (Clew)

Jim Redman – 6 Times World Motorcycle Champion: The Autobiography (Redman)
'Sox' – Gary Hocking – the forgotten World Motorcycle Champion (Hughes)

General
BMW Boxer Twins 1970-1995 Bible, The (Falloon)
BMW Cafe Racers (Cloesen)
BMW Custom Motorcycles – Choppers, Cruisers, Bobbers, Trikes & Quads (Cloesen)
Bonjour – Is this Italy? (Turner)
British 250cc Racing Motorcycles (Pereira)
British Café Racers (Cloesen)
British Custom Motorcycles – The Brit Chop – choppers, cruisers, bobbers & trikes (Cloesen)
BSA Bantam Bible, The (Henshaw)
BSA Motorcycles – the final evolution (Jones)
Ducati 750 Bible, The (Falloon)
Ducati 750 SS 'round-case' 1974, The Book of the (Falloon)
Ducati 860, 900 and Mille Bible, The (Falloon)
Ducati Monster Bible (New Updated & Revised Edition), The (Falloon)
Ducati 916 (updated edition) (Falloon)
Fine Art of the Motorcycle Engine, The (Peirce)
From Crystal Palace to Red Square – A Hapless Biker's Road to Russia (Turner)
Funky Mopeds (Skelton)
How to Restore Classic Off-road Motorcycles (Burns)
Italian Cafe Racers (Cloesen)
Italian Custom Motorcycles (Cloesen)
Japanese Custom Motorcycles – The Nippon Chop – Chopper, Cruiser, Bobber, Trikes & Quads (Cloesen)
Kawasaki Triples Bible, The (Walker)
Kawasaki Z1 Story, The (Sheehan)
Lambretta Bible, The (Davies)
Laverda Twins & Triples Bible 1968-1986 (Falloon)
Little book of trikes, the (Quellin)
Morgan 3 Wheeler – back to the future!, The (Dron)
Moto Guzzi Sport & Le Mans Bible, The (Falloon)
Motorcycle Apprentice (Cakebread)
Motorcycle GP Racing in the 1960s (Pereira)
Motorcycle Road & Racing Chassis Designs (Noakes)
MV Agusta Fours, The book of the classic (Falloon)
Norton Command Bible, The (Henshaw)
Off-Road Giants! (Volume 1) – Heroes of 1960s Motorcycle Sport (Westlake)
Off-Road Giants! (Volume 2) – Heroes of 1960s Motorcycle Sport (Westlake)
Off-Road Giants! (volume 3) – Heroes of 1960s Motorcycle Sport (Westlake)
Racing Line – British motorcycle racing in the golden age of the big single (Guntrip)
Scooters & Microcars, The A-Z of Popular (Dan)
Scooter Lifestyle (Grainger)
SCOOTER MANIA! – Recollections of the Isle of Man International Scooter Rally (Jackson)
Triumph Bonneville Bible (59-83) (Henshaw)
Triumph Bonneville!, Save the – The inside story of the Meriden Workers' Co-op (Rosamond)
Triumph Motorcycles & the Meriden Factory (Hancox)
Triumph Speed Twin & Thunderbird Bible (Woolridge)
Triumph Tiger Cub Bible (Estall)
Triumph Trophy Bible (Woolridge)
TT Talking – The TT's most exciting era – As seen by Manx Radio TT's lead commentator 2004-2012 (Lambert)
Velocette Motorcycles – MSS to Thruxton – New Third Edition (Burris)
Vespa – The Story of a Cult Classic in Pictures (Uhlig)
Vincent Motorcycles: The Untold Story since 1946 (Guyony & Parker)

www.veloce.co.uk

For post publication news, updates and amendments relating to this book please visit www.veloce.co.uk/books/V4896

First published August 2016 by Veloce Publishing Limited, Veloce House, Parkway Farm Business Park, Middle Farm Way, Poundbury, Dorchester, Dorset, DT1 3AR, England. Fax 01305 250479/e-mail info@veloce.co.uk/web www.veloce.co.uk or www.velocebooks.com.

ISBN: 978-1-845848-96-5 UPC: 6-36847-04896-9

BRITISH
CAFÉ RACERS

Uli Cloesen

VELOCE PUBLISHING
THE PUBLISHER OF FINE AUTOMOTIVE BOOKS

Contents

Introduction

I am the first to admit, I love the Isle of Man. It really is the Mecca for everyone even only slightly interested in motorcycles and racing, coupled with friendly locals and stunning scenery, although a bit far from New Zealand's shores. So when I had the chance to attend the Classic TT race week during a 2015 trip to the UK, I jumped at the opportunity. What's there to say: I was not disappointed. As soon as I left the airport, and throughout the week, the variety of encounters with racing bikes, road bikes, café racers, along with their respective pilots on the island, was just staggering. Upon returning home, the idea grew to conceptualise a book which looked at British motorcycles that shaped the café racer era, from its inception right through to the present day, alongside the racing bikes the café racer culture drew its inspiration from. The result is now in front of you, I hope you like it.

Uli Cloesen

ACKNOWLEDGEMENTS

The author and publisher wish to acknowledge their debt to all who contributed material and photographs for this book.

The majority of the images in this work stem from the author's collection.

www.ulicloesen.com

Previous page: Ex-motorcycle GP technician Jason Hall's Café Racer café in Wellington, NZ.

Dave Mead's badged jacket reads like a roll call of classic British café racers. (See page 73.)

CHAPTER 1
AJS TO BSA

AJS

Associated Motor Cycles introduced its AJS 7R racing motorcycle in 1948. It provided plenty of inspiration for the 'going fast brigade,' be they factory or privateer riders. The bike, with its chain-driven overhead-camshaft, designed by Phil Walker, was historically related to AJS' prewar 'cammy' single-cylinder bikes. The 350cc four-stroke racer initially produced 32hp @ 7500rpm, slightly down on power to its competition. This led, in 1951, to engineer Ike Hatch developing a three-valve head version of the 7R, increasing its output to 36hp, to better compete against its Italian multi-cylinder foes. Works team leader, Jack Williams, then managed to bring the engine up to 40hp in 1954, but increasing competition led AMC to withdraw from racing at the end of that year. Thereafter, AJS produced the two-valve 7R for privateers, alongside a 500cc version badged as a Matchless G50, until the end of production in 1963.

The AJS 7R won the Junior Manx TT from 1961-1963. It had a top speed of 115-120mph (180-190km/h), tipping the scales at a mere 129kg.

Bill James' 1954 AJS 7R 350 is prepared to compete in the 2015 Burt Munro Challenge Invercargill Street Races, NZ.

The AJS 7R was commonly named the 'Boy Racer.'

ARIEL

In his 1988 book *Café Racer*, Mike Clay remembers a chap named Peter Ferbrache riding a stripped down 1935 Ariel Red Hunter in the early '50s as one of the finest café racers of all time. He termed this rider's bike a 'Street Sleeper,' tuned for racing by Laurence Hartley, and described by Clay as capable of blowing any normal bike clean off the road during a match race wager in the UK's Epping Forest area, back in its day. This provided the impetus to look for more Red Hunter caffs, leading to finding Spaniard Oliver Naranjo's fine example here.

The Birmingham-built Ariel Red Hunter overhead-valve singles were designed by Val Page in 1932, in 250, 350 and 500cc displacements,

The Ariel NH Red Hunter 500, with a 1932 engine, strikes a nice pose. Café features include Ace bars and humped seat.

and gained popularity with off-road riders. Edward Turner later added his touch to the bike, making it popular with touring road riders also.

It's claimed that a 500cc Red Hunter could reach 0-60mph in 10.9 seconds. From 1955, racing legend Sammy Miller successfully championed a 500cc Red Hunter. The production run ended in 1959.

Lastly, for good measure, a 1950s Ariel Red Hunter 500cc racer seen at the Festival of Motorcycling 2015, in Jurby, Isle of Man.

Ready for action for a run on the old RAF airfield track.

NORIEL 4 CAFÉ RACER

Ariel produced its Square Four model between 1931 and 1959. Its one-litre four-stroke engine received a further lease of life in the Healey 1000-4 Special, based on an updated Square Four motor and a new frame, produced in limited quantity by the Healey brothers between 1971 and 1977.

The 997cc (60.8in³) Café Racer Special below, powered by a modified Ariel Square Four engine, is on display at the Bicheno Motorcycle Museum in Tasmania, Australia. The bike was built in 2000 for an English client and sports a Norton Featherbed frame, Norton gearbox, and Norton Manx tank. Everything else on it is hand-made.

The custom hybrid captured photographer Lawson Harding's imagination. He has a soft spot for Ariels, as his grandfather was the Tasmanian Ariel agent between the 1920s and 1950s.

The standard Mark II engines were built from 1953–1959 and produced 40hp (30kW) @ 5800rpm, and were capable of 100mph (160km/h). (Courtesy Lawson Harding)

The exhaust system is custom-made. (Courtesy Lawson Harding)

Noriel transfer close-up. (Courtesy Lawson Harding)

Another display, at the Antique & Vintage Fair in Hobart, Tasmania.
(Courtesy John T)

The 250cc two-stroke Ariel Leader, designed by Val Page and Bernard Knight, was launched in 1958 and was produced until 1965. The fully enclosed bike lent itself to sportier duties, too, although relieved of its bodywork, as shown here.

A 250cc Ariel Leader two-stroke racer at the 2011 Thundersprint in Northwich, UK. (Courtesy James Halbery)

Also worth mentioning is the 200cc Ariel Arrow, a more affordable, stripped Leader, which was developed into the Golden Arrow 'Sport' variant in 1963.

BSA

The BSA Gold Star was, in the '50s, the bike to aspire to, to hit the magic 'ton' – 100mph (160.9km/h). The model's story dates back to 1937, when Wal Handley, after riding a BSA Empire Star around the Brooklands circuit at over 100mph, excited BSA bosses enough to produce the Gold Star model.

The first version, coded M24 up until the outbreak of World War Two, had a 28hp alloy 496cc engine, coupled to an Electron alloy gearbox. The B32 Gold Star 348cc was launched after the conflict. Once a buyer decided between a touring, off-road, or the – for the café racer cult – relevant Clubman trim, the bikes were then hand assembled and the engine bench tested in the factory. The differences between the smaller Goldie and the 499cc B34 model were found in the main bearing design and crankshaft configuration. The larger Gold Star received a new cylinder head from 1952 onwards, with the 350cc model following suit the year after. This was followed by a re-worked gearbox and the start of the swing-arm duplex frame. Any buyer asking for Clubman cams and timing in 1955 also received

a special silencer. The same year also saw Eddie Dow winning the Senior Clubmans TT on a BSA Gold Star.

The DBD34 500cc model from 1956 produced 40hp @ 7000rpm, with a bore x stroke of 85x88mm. It could reach 110mph (180km/h) and was fitted with a chrome-plated fuel tank, clip-on bars, an alloy engine with 36mm Amal carb, and a swept-back exhaust. Faults with Gold Stars were few, notably the Lucas magdyno and a tendency to jump out of second gear. Gold Star production finally ended in 1963.

A Gold Star parked in Douglas, IoM.

The Goldie with its trademark chrome fuel tank.

In 2015, the UK branch of the Gold Star Owners Club celebrated its 40th Anniversary. The main club event took place at the Manx Classic TT, on the Isle of Man, with over 170 members and approximately 100 Goldies having taken part in the week of events.

Below is some author's footage of the Goldie descent on the Isle of Man.

Naturally there were also some Goldie specials parked on the Island.

Goldie pilots waiting for access to the Jurby race track.

The heart of the matter.

BSA Goldie Run, parked at the VMCC Rally in Tynwald.

Gold Star with Ace Café logo.

View from the top.

This beauty was amongst the Goldie lineup in Jurby.

View from the front.

Above: Isn't she a beauty?!
Left: The Tempest at Cadwell Park in 2012.
It produces 46hp @ 7200rpm and a top
speed of 125mph. (Courtesy Julie Steele)
Below: On display at the 2015 VMCC
Tynwald gathering.

David Steele's 500cc 2003 Tonkin Tempest is another Goldie special spotted at the VMCC Tynwald event. His bike sports a Gold Star DBD34 engine in a Seeley Mk3 replica frame by Roger Titchmarsh. The OHV two-valve four-stroke single-cylinder motor is built by ABSAF (Dutch-built BSA Gold Star replica) and has a bore x stroke of 85x88mm, with a compression ratio of 9:1. Suspension at the front is a 35mm Ceriani fork, at the rear, a swinging arm with NJB shocks. The carburettor consists of an Amal GP 1.5in (38mm) item, and transmission is taken care of by a Tonkin dry belt primary, and chain final drive. The gearbox is a RRT2 Tonkin five-speed and the front brake is a Lockheed 10in single disc with Grimeca master cylinder.

The rear brake consists of an SLS in a Triumph 7in conical hub. Tyres are Avon Road Riders rubber, 90x90-18 front, and 100x90-18 rear. The Tempest fuel tank holds 4 UK gallons (18 litres).

David can't remember how he got into the café racer days, it was so long ago. However, he remembered when he chose to enter his first short circuit club road-race event in 1965. He didn't have much money and no means of getting to the Oulton Park circuit, because the machine (a Gold Star DBD34 engine in a Dominator wide-line frame), had no lights and the journey (some eighty-odd miles) meant starting out before daylight. However, his best mate had a Triumph Herald car and he suggested take out the back seats, and the bike could go in the boot and the wheels would fit-in where the seats had been. Easy does it!

Tonkin Tempest builder Steve Tonkin has over 20 years experience as an expert restorer and builder of new hand-crafted bikes under his belt. He learned to ride on Matchless and Velocette bikes, and started racing Nortons in the '70s. A change to Yamaha strokers earned him six placings at the Isle of Man TT, and a win at the 250cc Junior TT in 1981. He also won the British 250 Championship between 1980 and 1982, finally retiring from racing in 1984. He now focuses on producing modern café racing machinery.

The following bike was crafted in Spain from leftover pieces of a 1968 BSA Bantam 175 D10 restoration.

The BSA Bantam lightweight single-cylinder two-stroke was built in large numbers during its production run, from 1948 (initially as a 125cc version) until 1971 (with a 175cc displacement). The design was actually based on the German DKW RT125, and obtained as part of the war reparations. The RT125 is considered the most copied motorcycle in the world. The differences from the original design was a right-side gear change, imperial fixings, and right-hand side controls, to match British conditions at the time.

The Bantam in its original livery. It had an output of 10hp and a top speed of 57mph (92km/h). (Courtesy Oliver Naranjo)

The Bantam racer on a Spanish plaza ... she's looking rather good! (Courtesy Oliver Naranjo)

The BSA Super Rocket was the result of the Birmingham firm's development of the BSA Road Rocket. The company's A10 model was considered reliable, but falling behind its Norton and Triumph competition. The Super Rocket was released in 1957 in an attempt to address this, with a new alloy head and an Amal TT racing carburettor. In 1961 a new high-lift camshaft was introduced to improve performance.

Its 650cc 46-50hp Rocket Gold Star 'Clubman' version (depending on specs) was built from 1961-63, and was fitted with a tuned A10 Super Rocket engine, based on modifications by Eddie Dow. It also had a double downtube Gold Star frame and a dry weight of 170kg.

A Super Rocket on the Jurby car park at the IoM. Right: Super Rocket launcher logo.

A black Super Rocket on display in Tynwald ...

.. complete with rear sets, clip-on handlebars and swept-back exhausts.

A badge for the true fan.

The BSA A10 RGS in all its glory.
(Courtesy www.ventureclassics.co.uk)

CHAPTER 2

BROUGH SUPERIOR TO MATCHLESS

BROUGH SUPERIOR

Brough Superior motorcycles are considered the Rolls-Royce of the biking world, with prices to match. They were also fast, with George Brough lapping the Brooklands circuit at 100mph (160km/h) on his first side-valve bike as early as 1922, and Eric Fernihough achieving a Motorcycle Land Speed Record for the flying kilometre at 169.8mph (273.3km/h) in 1937

Brough Superior café racers don't exist to my knowledge, but imagine the Manx Superior racer below as a road-going caff.

Ewan Cameron, from Cameron Engineering & Motorsport Ltd in Malvern, Worcestershire, lives and breathes JAP engines and motorsport. He originally built the bike below circa 2006, along with another one that his brother sold to a French museum. The racer sports a 1947 all-alloy JAP Mk1 Type Two engine (originally designed for the 1100cc F2 Cooper racing car), fitted into a 1956 Manx Norton frame. This particular motor was used in a racing Brough Superior during the 1960s, hence Ewan named the bike the 'Manx Superior.' He continually improved it and developed it into a formidable racing machine. Ewan built the bike to compete in British Classic Formula 1. His ambition is to race it at the Isle of Man Classic F1 TT.

There are, however, some individuals who put JAP engines into road-going frames, like the JAP BSA special from Australia, above right, courtesy of JAP expert Greg Summerton.

Colin Sunderland's JAP BSA. (Courtesy Greg Summerton)

JAP (short for JA Prestwich, of Tottenham, London) engineered motors were, apart from Brough Superior, also used in Triumph, Enfield Cycle Co, AJ Stevens & Co Ltd, Zenith, HRD and some German- and French-built motorcycles.

New Cameron Engineering internals, 90x99mm, 1260cc, two 34mm Amal smooth-bore carbs, twin-plug electronic ignition, Japanese 38mm forks and twin-disc 19in wheel AP racing calipers at the front, oval swinging arm and 18in rear Manx wheel at the back.
(Courtesy Ewan Cameron)

COTTON

The 1919-founded Gloucester-based manufacturer launched a new series of road bikes in 1954, some of which were also used by the café brigade. Its Villiers-powered competition motorcycles were very successful through the '60s, especially so with Derek Minter at the helm of a Villiers Starmaker-engined Cotton Telstar. Proof of the Telstar's potential was documented by Minter's ninth position in the 1965 Lightweight, at an average speed of 84mph (135km/h). The company closed its doors in the '80s, marking over 60 years of motorcycle production. Cotton enthusiasts celebrated at the Brooklands museum in 2014, the centenary of Frank Willoughby Cotton's 1914 patented triangulated frame that formed the basis of the early Cotton Motorcycles. Below are some examples of Cotton machinery.

EXCELSIOR

The next historic sporting machine stems from Coventry firm Bayliss, Thomas and Co, Britain's first bike builders. The company created the Excelsior brand in 1910 and used engines from Blackburne, JAP, and Villiers to power its products. Racing improves the breed, so after initially trialing a Blackburne-sourced four-valve pushrod-operated racing engine in 1933, Excelsior created, with its Manxman model, a simpler and sturdier design in-house. This model was subsequently produced in capacities of 249, 348 and 498cc displacements. The Manxman was well received in the marketplace, with a reputation for reliability, and quite successful in international racing and on the Manx Grand Prix course. Production was stopped by World War Two and did not resume. Excelsior closed its doors in 1965.

A 1960s 247cc Cotton Conquest at the Centenary Rally in 2014. (Courtesy Richard Jones)

This bike, also at the 2014 Centenary Rally, is based on the AJS Stormer. (Courtesy Richard Jones)

Isle of Man logo on the engine casing. (Courtesy Yesterdays NL)

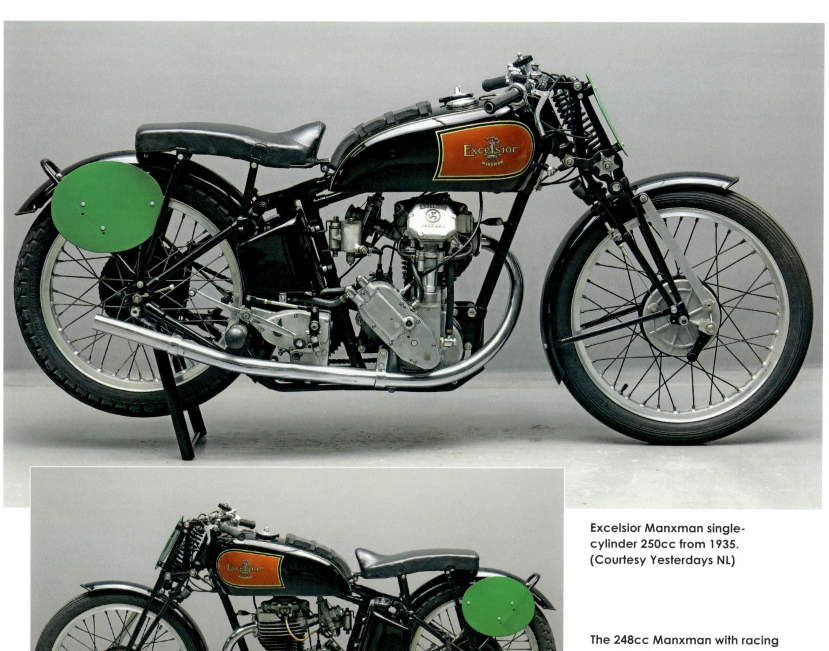

Excelsior Manxman single-cylinder 250cc from 1935. (Courtesy Yesterdays NL)

The 248cc Manxman with racing specifications won many races in its day.

The 1930 Excelsior JAP 'Silver Comet' on display.
(Sammy Miller Museum)

Don't you love the cockpit fairing on the world record-breaking Excelsior, left? The JAP-powered two-speed 1000cc supercharged racer hit 163mph (262km/h) in 1930, on the Tat motorway in Hungary, under rider Joe Wright. It's a case of form meets function.

HARLEY CR

In contrast to the Excelsior Silver Comet from the thirties is, perhaps, this 2015 Harley café racer as its modern V-twin counterpart, built by Peter Sutton and Andy Marsden under the Sutton & Marsden S&S Café Racers brand.

The bike sports a 1600cc S&S engine with 100hp, fitted into a replica Norton Featherbed frame. The motor is mated to a Norton gearbox that's been set up with Quaife internals. Primary drive is a Bob Newby clutch, and its belt drive kit was originally designed for a Manx Norton. The modified alloy fuel tank is handmade, and the bike sports Ducati top specification chassis components, Brembo braking, and Nitron – or optionally Öhlins – suspension. The bike, with its race-bred handling and braking, is intended to update the old Triton philosophy.

Plenty of trickery on the Harley CR seen at Jurby, IoM.

GREEVES

Bert Greeves started the Invacar brand in 1951, producing three-wheeled invalid cars. He soon ventured into motorcycles as well, manufacturing scrambler and road bikes from autumn 1953 onwards, intended as a sideline for the company.

Greeves off-road bikes stamped their mark in the trials market against its British competition. Its Ranger road legal off-roader was quite influential in the United States as well. In 1956 Greeves signed motocross rider and two-stroke tuning specialist Brian Stonebridge, which improved the performance of the Villiers engines significantly, leading to race wins in 1957 and in turn establishing Greeves' reputation as a true off-road competition motorcycle manufacturer.

The company also made successful inroads into road racing with its 250cc Silverstone model, produced from 1963 (Mk1 version) to 1968 (Mk5 version). With its reputation for reliability, it sold dozens of Silverstone bikes to club racers in the 250cc class.

At the 1964 Manx Grand Prix, Gordon Keith wrung his Greeves racer in the last lap of the four-lap race to 87.6mph (141km/h), marking the best speed ever by a British 250cc motorcycle. In 1966, Peter Inchley then bettered this achievement when he lapped the Manx course on a Villiers Starmaker Special at 93.17mph (149.94km/h).

GREEVES' & COTTON'S USE OF VILLIERS ENGINES

Villiers engineering was based in Wolverhampton, England. The company produced its first 350cc four-stroke engine as early as 1912. From 1914 onwards, its 269cc two-stroke motor had already been adopted by a large number of motorcycle manufacturers. Villiers produced munitions during World War One, but patented the flywheel-magneto in 1917, to overcome the British bike industries' need for previously German-sourced magnetos. After the war, Villiers resumed its supply of 269cc engine to various manufacturers. Fast-forward to World War Two, and Villiers again engaged in making munitions, but this time alongside production of engines and cycle parts. By 1956, Villiers rolled out its two-millionth engine! In an expansion move, the company absorbed JA Prestwich in 1957, in an attempt to encapsulate the British market more comprehensively. Until the 1960s, Villiers produced two-stroke motorcycle engines ranging from 98cc to 325cc displacements for various manufacturers. From the early '60s on, the company underwent several takeovers, until it became Norton-Villiers-Triumph in 1972, which folded in 1978.

Greeves 24RAS Silverstone MkI from 1963, on display at the Burley in Wharfedale Classic Vehicle Show, August 2014: a lovely classic '60s British racer. (Courtesy Steve Glover)

MATCHLESS

Henry Collier & Sons founded Matchless in 1899 and produced its own engines from 1912 on. The marque's offerings, manufactured in Plumstead, London, ranged from small capacity two-strokes to 750cc four-stroke twins. The company was amalgamated into Associated Motorcycles in 1938, together with AJS, but both brands continued models under their respective names. Matchless also supplied V-twin engines to Morgan and Brough Superior. The company has a long history of racing success, and its bikes are still alive and kicking in today's classic racing events. Its G50 single cylinder racer was made available for privateers in 1959, with its main rival having been the Norton Manx. Matchless production folded in 1966.

WALMSLEY MATCHLESS RACER

Malcolm Potter's fabulous looking 1962 Matchless G50 was built by Fred Walmsley. The bike was on racing duty in 2011 at Goodwood under Scott Smart, and also competed in the Lansdown Championship in 2012 with Glen English, achieving second in the race. Wayne Gardner and Luke Notton also rode it, in 2013 at the Goodwood Festival, in the Barry Sheene Memorial trophy, finishing in sixth place.

The 500cc engine produces 56hp @ 8200rpm.

This Seeley Matchless MkII is a fine example of Colin's innovative and successful bikes.

SEELEY MATCHLESS 500

Colin Seeley started racing motorcycles in 1954, and from 1961 onwards became a well-known sidecar racer, using Matchless, Norton, and BMW engines for his outfits. At the end of 1966, Seeley bought the AMC race shop, as he wanted to concentrate on the Matchless G50 and AJS 7R machines. He retired from racing in 1967 and subsequently turned his attention to building racing bikes, using his own frame design.

His first prototype framework consisted of Reynolds 531 tubing, and turned out to be over four kilograms lighter than the Matchless G50 frame.

Seeley's prototype frame was fitted with a Manx Norton fork, swingarm, and a conical Manx rear hub. His later frames featured his own swingarm; a gearbox with either four, five, or six gears could also be had, subject to customer requirements. Seeley worked out of Belvedere, Kent, until 1979.

Gearbox is a six-speed Hemmings cassette, mated to a Newby belt drive and clutch, while the engine is a 90x78mm bore x stroke twin spark, with a special one-piece crank, titanium conrod, and two-ring slipper piston.

In the pit lane in Jurby, Isle of Man.

Closeup of tank and head stock.

Another view of engine and framework.

SURTEES MATCHLESS

Next is a 1962 Matchless G50 racer, built by four-time 500cc motorcycle World Champion John Surtees. The frame for this special was his own design, blending the best features of a Norton Featherbed frame with a Matchless G50 chassis. Surtees made extensive use of magnesium alloy and titanium, with the intention of making this bike as light as possible. It's on display at the Barber Motorsports Museum, Birmingham, Alabama.

The 496cc single-cylinder engine puts out 55hp @ 7200rpm, has a bore and stroke of 90x78mm, and is fed by a single magnesium alloy Amal GP carburettor.

Ceriani telescopic front forks; front brakes are four-leading-shoe drum, rear are Norton Manx drum; weight is 245lb (111kg).
(Courtesy Michael Bufkin)

TONKIN TYPHOON MATCHLESS

Lastly, we move from racers to café racers again. David Steele's air-cooled OHC four-stroke two-valve single-cylinder Matchless G50 café racer, left, was built in 2003 by Steve Tonkin. The 50hp engine has a bore x stroke of 90x78mm and a capacity of 496cc. The compression ratio is 10:1 and lubrication is by dry sump. The engine breathes through a Mikuni 38mm Amal MkII Concentric carburettor, and is housed in a Seeley Mk3 Replica frame by Roger Titchmarsh.

The transmission consists of a Tonkin dry belt primary and a chain final drive (Norton Commando clutch cover), and the gearbox is an RRT2 Tonkin five-speed with dry multi-plate clutch. The suspension at the front is 35mm Ceriani forks. and at the rear, a swinging arm with NJB shocks. The four-leading-shoe drum front brakes are also from Ceriani, the rear being a single-leading-shoe in a BSA/Triumph conical hub. Tyres are Avon Road Riders: front 90x90-18, rear 100x90-18. Seat height comes to 29½in (750mm) and the bike holds four UK gallons (18 litres) of fuel. Lastly, top speed is an estimated 135mph (217km/h).

This is just the perfect toy for a few fast hours on a sunny weekend. (Courtesy Julie Steele)

CHAPTER 3
NORTON

NORTON

James Lansdowne Norton founded Norton in 1898 in Birmingham, England. His company began building bikes in 1902, initially with bought-in engines. The first Norton-made motor surfaced in 1908, marking the beginning of a long line of fine motorcycles, and with it, much racing success.

In fact, Norton won 43 TT races between its first TT event in 1907 and 1992, which is an achievement it can be proud of. Its Norton Manx singles were dominant in the late '50s and early '60s, right in the heyday of café racer culture. The use of the Manx name stems from the racing version of Norton's International roadster, the Manx Grand Prix model, in service from 1936 until 1940.

From 1947 onwards, the Norton single racer was simply called the Manx, omitting the Grand Prix portion of its name. The Manx Norton was produced in 350cc (40M) and 500cc (30M) guise as a long stroke version until 1953, then changed to a short stroke version until 1962. It can still be bought new from several suppliers around the globe.

Geoff Duke signed with Norton as a works rider in 1950. The same year saw the appearance of the Belfast-based McCandless brothers-designed Featherbed frame, a chassis which offered a significant weight reduction and greatly improved handling compared to its 'garden gate' termed predecessor.

The front fork geometry and rear shock absorbers were also made by McCandless, with a built-in reservoir to stop the oil overheating and cavitating. Duke subsequently claimed the Senior TT in 1950-51 on the Manx Norton. He considered the Featherbed-fitted Manx the best handling motorcycle he ever rode.

The below bike is the only surviving 1950 Works Norton, owned by Peter Bloore and meticulously restored in New Zealand by Ken McIntosh of McIntosh Racing.

This Norton Manx is a 1939 model ...

... on display in Douglas, IoM.

A piece of history: the 1950 works Norton, with the Senior TT Trophy in the foreground. (Courtesy Ken McIntosh)

Front and rear of a concours 500cc Norton Manx 30M from 1958, owned by Malcolm Potter.

The opposite page shows a late '50s Norton Manx, on display in Tynwald, IoM. A 500cc Manx could exceed a top speed of 130mph (210km/h), with a dry weight of 140kg.

The silver Norton racer, shown below, competed in the Isle of Man 2015 Classic TT.

Colin Seeley bought the remainder of the Norton spares and tools in 1966, which he later sold to John Tickle in 1969. Tickle then built the Manx T5 500 and T3 350 coded racers, using the short-stroke Manx engines. He also moved his stock and rights on to Unity Equipe in the late '70s. Fast forward to 1994, and Preston-based Andy Molnar took over the manufacturing rights, initially producing parts in line with Norton's 1961 drawings, but then following this with complete engines, and ultimately leading to the manufacture of his own Molnar Manx bikes. Steve Tonkin, mentioned earlier in the book, also produces a road version of the Manx, entitled the Tonkin Tornado.

Manx Norton engines also had a major impact on the rise of postwar car racing. Towards the end of the '50s, when 500cc Formula 3 gained momentum, the Manx engine became the power plant everyone was vying for. The only trouble was that Norton would only sell complete bikes; hence many punters bought a Manx just for its engine, with the rest being surplus to requirements. This opened

Norton Lowboy International 500 from 1959, owned by George Cohen.

A Molnar engine closeup.

Not an ounce of fat on this bike.

The Molnar Manx ready for track duty.

up opportunities for getting hold of the best reputed road holding frames available for motorcycles, and pairing them with the best Triumph engines considered for fast use on the road, and, alas, the Triton was born. But the Triton was not the only hybrid out there.

To start to illustrate this point, see the Norton Jawa Special, next. This racer consists of a 500cc Methanol-fed Jawa Speedway engine, fitted into a slightly modified Norton Wideline Featherbed frame. Other Norton items used are its four-speed gearbox, an early Commando twin-leading-shoe front brake and Roadholder front forks. A Mick Hemmings swinging arm and a BSA/Triumph rear conical hub can also be found, alongside yolks machined from alloy billets, and many other hand-made parts, such as engine plates, clip-on brackets, and foot pegs.

The Norton Jawa in 2015, in the pit lane at Jurby, IoM. David McCoy also raced this Special at Olivers Mount and Darley Moor, among others.

Norton's Dominator twin-cylinder model was released in 1949, designed by Bert Hopwood and aimed to take some sales away from Triumph's Speed Twin. Norton's works racing team temporarily used race-tuned Dominators from 1960, but they were still outperformed by its own Norton Manx. This prompted Doug Hele to produce a 55hp Domiracer, while saving 16kg in weight over the Manx in the process. As a result, Dennis Greenfield and Fred Swift won the 500cc class in the Thruxton 500 race in 1960. In 1961 Tom Phillis managed third place in the IoM TT, lapping at over 100mph (161km/h), which marked a first for any twin.

Above: A Norton Domiracer being readied for action. **Inset:** Closeup of the bike's front section.

A Dunstall Norton at a 2011 Britbike Rally in Juva, Finland. (Courtesy Jojje Kontio)

Norton abandoned the Domiracer project in 1962 with the closure of its race shop. The racer and factory parts were then acquired by Paul Dunstall, who carried on with further development. Dunstall then made a name for himself fabricating Norton performance parts and, in due course, producing his Dunstall Norton bikes.

Left and below: A Norton 750 Café Racer parked at a petrol station in Ramsey. She's a nice-looking mount.

This beauty was parked near the Jurby Transport Museum.

Although Tritons ruled the roost in the '60s, this doesn't mean that all-out Norton-based café racers were something to be sneered at, as the following selection demonstrates nicely. Norton produced the Commando, with its 745cc OHV parallel-twin engine, from 1967 until 1973. Thereafter, its displacement was lifted to 828cc until the end of its production run in 1977. The 750cc factory spec Commando was good for 115mph (185km/h), and so well regarded that the UK's *Motorcycle News* bestowed on it the Machine of the Year title five years in a row, from 1968-1972.

Another nice Norton café example, with its period swept-back exhausts.

NORTON COMMANDO RACING

Soon after its inception in 1967, the Commando was entered in racing events. After some success by Norton dealer-entered machines (such as Paul Smart's second place in the Isle of Man TT Production class in 1969) Norton resolved to make a racing version, producing the S and Yellow Peril models. A period test attested a 1971 Norton Commando Production Racer a top Speed of 131mph (210.82km/h). Although it came equipped with lights and was fully street legal, this bike was never really intended for the street. This could be the real thing, below.

Norton then formed a racing team at the Thruxton circuit from late 1971 onwards, with backing from sponsor and cigarette maker John Player. Two new bikes were finished in time for the Daytona

This beauty was parked at the back of the Jurby pit lane.

200 mile event in March 1972. The below machine with number 22 achieved fourth place there, ridden by World Champion Phil Read. This blue racer (along with the white version) is part of the UK's National Motorcycle Museum collection. Fast-forward to the Isle of Man Festival of Jurby 2015, where a Norton Commando special can still strut its stuff on the old RAF race track.

Thanks to wind tunnel-developed streamlining, the 1972 F750 Combat engine hit the Daytona speed trap at 152.54mph (245.49km/H).

Above: Stephen Bardwell's 1972 Norton Seeley 750 racer.

This white 749cc John Player Norton was raced by development rider Peter Williams under Number 11, on which he won the Production race of the 1973 Silverstone Hutchinson 100 event. As Number 2, it replicates the Thruxton Isle of Man trim, fitted with a large fuel tank and lighting.

'There are no substitutes for cubes' or 'there's no replacement for displacement' is Steve Maney's approach to making a Norton Commando faster. In 2003 he created the World's largest capacity Norton engine, dishing out 1007cc. It's not just an over-bored 850cc Commando engine; all the engine internals have been redesigned to accommodate the larger bore and stroke. Steve's engineering shop in Wakefield manufactures a complete kit to convert one's 750/850 Commando motor into his Maney 1007cc engine.

But let's come briefly back to Racing Nortons. When Norton Villiers amalgamated with BSA-Triumph to create NVT, it meant the end of factory racing. Production of the Norton Commando ended in 1977, but from 1987 onwards, the Norton badge re-appeared on the limited production 588cc air-cooled twin-rotor Wankel engine-powered Classic model, developed by David Garside (later succeeded by the liquid-cooled Norton Commander). Norton re-ignited the racing chapter from 1987 to 1994, competing in International Road races, the British Superbike Championship (won by Steve Spray on a JPS Norton in 1989 and Ian Simpson on the Duckhams Norton in 1994), and on the Isle of Man. Steve Hislop's famous win on a number 19 position ABUS Norton, over Carl Fogarty riding a Yamaha, in the Senior TT in 1992 marked the last time a rotary Norton raced around the TT course. It was therefore extra special to witness the 2015 Isle of Man Classic TT Norton – The Rotary Years – Parade, where punters had a chance to see thirteen rotary racers lap the mountain course, again in unison (some of them ridden by their original riders), machines owned and prepared by the UK's National Motorcycle Museum.

The engine puts out 97hp on the dyno and has a 83x93mm bore x stroke: this Maney Norton packs serious power.

The JPS Rotary Norton used by Robert Dunlop, with Trevor Nation's ex bike behind it.

Steve Hislop's Number 19 Norton Rotary.

A rotary racer with its fairing stripped.

The new Norton venture under Stuart Garner set up shop in Donington Park in 2008. Its first modern Commando 961SE model rolled out in 2010, which heralded the glorious marque's return to production. In 2009, Stuart Garner set a 173mph World Record for a timed mile on a rotary-powered motorcycle, on a Norton NRV588, followed by a top speed in excess of 180mph. Currently, Norton produces three 961 Commando variants: the SF, Café Racer, and Sport models.

Lastly, in July 2015, Norton announced the first exports of the new Norton Dominator SS, bound for France and Australia, marking the return of a glorious name, and signifying a major step forward for Norton in expanding its model range beyond the Commando 961 platform. All Dominator SS bikes are hand-built in Donington Park, and feature an iconic Featherbed-styled chassis, hand-crafted aluminium fuel tank, and Öhlins suspension. They are the limited edition version of the Domiracer: a stock Dominator with a steel petrol tank instead of an aluminium item, which will be more widely available. Norton seems well on its way to a bright future again.

The 961cc air-cooled parallel-twin Café Racer has a compression ratio of 10:1 and a bore x stroke of 88x79mm. Valve actuation is by pushrod, with hydraulic lifters and two valves per cylinder. The bike is fitted with electronic fuel injection, and sports a stainless steel exhaust.

The big front disks with Brembo radial calipers should provide fierce stopping power to the 17in front wheel.

The 961cc air-cooled, parallel-twin, two-valve Dommie motor puts out 80hp, with a 8000rpm redline. Coupled with its race pipe, it should provide plenty of poke.

CHAPTER 4

ROYAL ENFIELD TO RUDGE

The Continental GT is available in red, yellow, or black and produces 29hp @ 5100rpm, with a top speed of 90mph (145km/h).

With its red glassfibre tank, fly screen, clip-on handlebars, swept pipe, and humped seat, the Continental GT, was a popular mount in its day – and looked every bit the racer. (Courtesy Roger Mills)

ROYAL ENFIELD

In the late '50s and early '60s the Redditch, Worcestershire-based Enfield Cycle Company produced several motorcycles with 250cc displacements to cater for the UK's important learner class, which didn't require a rider to pass a test. Its biggest seller was the 18hp pushrod OHV single-cylinder Crusader, but the 248cc Royal Enfield Continental GT, unveiled at the Earls Court Show in November 1964, really became a young rider's dream come true. This model, which drew inspiration from sporty Italian singles of the day, was essentially a factory-built café racer without any need for further customisation. The Continental GT produced 20hp @ 7500rpm, and presented itself as much like a racing bike as a road bike could possibly be; hence it won instant favour with its target audience.

In its August 1965 issue, *Motor Cycling* described the GT as the fastest British quarter-litre roadster they'd ever tested, with a best one-way speed of over 86mph (138.4km/h), coupled with confidence-inspiring, rock steady handling. For those in need, London dealers Deeprose Brothers and Gander & Gray produced some go-faster parts for the GT, with the latter offering a special version called the Gannet.

This bike differed in using a ported cylinder head with a larger inlet tract; fitted with a 10:1 piston, lead-bronze big-end shells, a full race fairing, and some alloy wheel rims. Unfortunately, 1967 marked the end of the Redditch factory, bringing a halt to the 250cc production. The Bradford-on-Avon factory then closed in 1970, heralding the end of the British Royal Enfield.

In 1954 Royal Enfield received an order from the Indian army to supply them with 800 350 Bullet singles. This in turn led, in 1956, to a joint venture between the British Enfield Cycle Company and the Indian Madras Motor Company. From then on, Enfield of India started building 350cc Bullets from UK components under license, and from the early '60s onwards, producing complete bikes. In 1995, the Indian company bought the rights to use the Royal Enfield name. Fast-forward to 2014, and Royal Enfield, under its dynamic CEO Sidharta Lal, released its homage to the Continental GT of old, the new 535cc Continental GT. The bike was penned by design firm Xenophya, while the twin-downtube cradle chassis was developed by Harris Performance, both from the UK. This collaboration resulted in an authentic looking Madras-built café racer with matching bloodlines.

This bike is fitted with a Motad stainless steel pipe and silencer, K&N air filter, Hagon rear shocks, a 40-tooth rear sprocket, a lighter rear chain, along with excess weight removal, and sports a modified Manx Norton fairing and low clip-ons.

CONTINENTAL GT RACER

The Continental GT, above, was purchased brand-new in 2014 as a Sunday morning toy, to give its owner Frank Jones' 1969 Bonneville (built with Thruxton legend George Hopwood to Thruxton factory racing specs) a rest from time to time. But, as he quotes, "Give an Englishman something that moves and he will race it," and this is exactly what happened.

The Royal Enfield was prepared as a production racer, which was then accepted by the VMCC as a 1965 'Replica' for parades and the like. Frank's first proper bike was a Ducati 175 Silverstone, from Kings of Oxford in 1963, which happened to be Mike Hailwood's dad's shop. He failed his first test on this bike: the examiner was GP Wold Champion Geoff Duke.

In 1966, his first British bike appeared, in the shape of a Triumph Tiger 90, with which he attended the local Rocker scene in Shrewsbury. In 1967 Frank managed to buy his dream bike, a nearly new Triumph Bonneville, which was promptly fitted with rear sets and Ace bars for its very first weekend run. He started racing in 1968 and continued until 1985, on bikes as diverse as his Thruxton-specced Bonnie, various Nortons, a Maico GP 125, a mean Kawasaki 750 Triple, followed by a Mick Walker Ducati 450 Special, a Dixon cantilever-framed Honda 500,

Frank lining up for the Jurby racetrack.

and Suzuki 500-750 hardware, after going through the Café Racer/ Rocker scene. Then, in 2007, he then started again for a 'one-off' to mark his 60th birthday, at the Thundersprint at Northwich, Cheshire, on a Storz Flattracker Harley 1200 Sportster. Frank now does mostly show events such as the Classic Parade on the Isle of Man. When asked who his café racer era inspiration was, he said Mike Hailwood, no contest!

The 1972 500cc Seeley-framed Royal Enfield Bullet racer parked in the pit lane in Douglas. Olie, Steve, and Ron Herring developed and manufactured a number of components for this machine.

Another Royal Enfield spotted on the Isle of Man in 2015, was the Flitwick Motorcycles/Steve Bond sponsored 500cc racer under rider Olie Linsdell, on duty in the Bennetts 500cc Classic TT race. The bike was built by Steve Linsdell, a man well renowned in the UK for his engineering and tuning skills. His exploits on Enfields turned the marque into one to be reckoned with. The Flitwick team are currently running the fastest racing Royal Enfield ever on the TT circuit.

Coming back to café racers, a nice fusion between old British Enfield and more recent Indian Enfield hardware can also be achieved, as the Royal Enfield café racers below demonstrate.

Hitchcock's Motorcycles is the place to go for café racer Enfield parts, notably their GT Café Racer kit or Continental kit with flyscreen. The company started in 1984, in a small unit in Redditch, the original home of Royal Enfield; now they are based in Solihull. In 1988, Hitchcock's bought Gander and Gray's stock, which supplied Royal Enfield parts and accessories since 1947, after its remaining founder Jack Gray went into retirement. Hitchcock's now has probably the globe's largest stock of spares, performance parts, and accessories for the Indian-made Bullets, as well as for the Redditch-based Royal Enfields from 1940 onwards. Watsonian Squire, which held the UK

In the Festival of Jurby bike parking area.

The Avon 'Speedflow' sports fairing fitted to this bike was available for the Continental GT model as an extra in complementary red and white factory colours.

The bike sports an Indian-built Lean Burn engine, first introduced to Britain in May 2002.

Another variation on the theme, the Royal Enfield Lean Burn engine café racer with a, presumably, Hitchcock's-supplied alloy fuel tank, parked near the Ramsay wharf.

The Royal Trifield, fitted with a 1965 Triumph T5 500cc motor ...

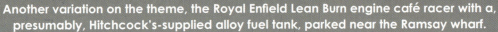

The logo says it all. (Courtesy Bob Lovelock)

distribution rights for Royal Enfield from 1999 to 2013 and still acts as an official RE dealer for the Cotswolds, also offered 500cc Clubman and Sportsman café racer versions, either with the classic four-speed iron barrel engine, or with the later five-speed Lean Burn power plant.

A rather nice-looking fusion between Royal Enfield and Triumph components is shown above-right. It's certainly not a common sight, but very well put together.

Royal Enfield twins also provided enough scope for customisation, albeit not so commonly seen.

Opposite is a late '50s Royal Enfield Super Meteor in standard guise, in contrast to a café'd Royal Enfield (the latter powered by either an early '60s Constellation or Super Meteor engine, judging by the splayed carbs), as seen on the Isle of Man.

... parked in Peterborough, August 2015.
(Courtesy Bob Lovelock)

Super Meteor: the heart of the matter.

Top: A Super Meteor parked near a VMCC gathering in Tynwald.
Bottom: The Royal Enfield caff in the Jurby bike parking area.

ROYAL ENFIELD 'GUNNER' CAFÉ RACER

Royal Enfield's Interceptor Series 1 was a successful move forward from the company's ill-reputed Constellation model, which had a reputation for blowing head gaskets, amongst other issues, rather than fitting the firm's 'Made like a Gun' slogan. The Interceptor's larger 736cc engine, with altered bore and stroke and new nodular iron crankshaft, was in response to American market wishes, aimed to compete against Norton's Atlas 750. The Interceptor was no slouch either, pumping out 52.5hp @ 6000rpm, with a top speed of 115mph (185km/h). So when Charles Giordano, from US firm Tailgunner Exhausts, in West Tisbury, MA, came across a 1968 Interceptor MkIA on its way to the scrap heap, the idea of a new custom project was born. What happens when a fine craftsman with a keen eye for design goes to work is ably demonstrated below. Not surprisingly, the Gunner was later found in *Cycle World* USA's Coolest Bikes 2015 award.

Left: Charles putting the Gunner through its paces. (Courtesy Bella Giordano)

Opposite page and left: The fuel tank is a Custom Manx-style replica: the seat consists of fibreglass and cork. The bottom of the front fork houses a wax-sealed Boston liniment bottle, holding a sailor's daily rum ration. The battery box is crafted from wooden cigar boxes. The burnt gases exit through a Tailgunner's Gatling gun-inspired rotating exhaust system. (Courtesy Charles F Giordano)

The latest iteration of the Carberry V-twin engine. (Courtesy Paul Carberry)

CARBERRY ENFIELD V-TWIN

Some time back, Australian Paul Carberry enlisted fellow countryman Ian Drysdale to develop an overhead-valve 55-degree 1000cc V-twin dry-sump four-stroke motor, out of two Royal Enfield single-cylinder engines. This subsequently went into limited production, but building complete V-twin bikes using predominantly Royal Enfield parts proved, ultimately, still too costly, so the venture closed its doors in Australia. But Carberry hasn't given up on his V-twin design, and has recently teamed up with Indian-based businessman Jaspreet Singh Bhatia to revive the project. This, in turn, led to Carberry relocating to India to set up manufacture there at much lower operating costs. Watch this space for an affordable, classic-looking V-twin appearing out of India in the near future.

RUDGE

Rudge-Whitworth resulted from the amalgamation of Whitworth Cycle Co, in Birmingham, and Rudge Cycle Co, from Coventry, in 1894. Its motorcycles were manufactured from 1911 to 1946, with the 499cc 45hp race replica overhead-valve single-cylinder Rudge Ulster, produced from 1929 to 1939, one of the company's most famous models. The name was a clever marketing ploy, celebrating Graham Walker's 1929 win at the Ulster GP. The depression resulted in the end of TT replicas and dirt bike production in 1933, but Rudge still managed to claim three podium places in the 1934 Lightweight TT. The company was taken over by EMI, which moved production to Middlesex in 1937. The onset of war in 1939 halted production.

The Carberry Enfield V-twin, here shown slotted into a highly modified 1995 Triumph frame. (Courtesy Paul Carberry)

Rhys Wilson's 1936 Rudge Ulster 500 racer at the 2015 Burt Munro Challenge Invercargill Street Race, NZ. The same bike and rider achieved second place at the Classic Pre '63 run of the 2015 Bluff Hillclimb event in NZ (right).

The 340 pound (154kg) dry weight special is fitted with Race 1.5in exhaust pipes with 'Harley style' absorption silencers, Triumph pre-unit gearbox with T140V five-speed internals and Triumph clutch, Ohlin adjustable hydraulic steering damper, Girling rear dampers, and Dunlop chromed steel 19in rims back and front. It boasts a Norton 1959 Wideline Featherbed frame, and swinging arm from a model 50, Suzuki GT750 four-leading-shoe front brake, rear Norton full-width hub single-leading-shoe brake, Suzuki GT750 front forks, shortened and machined to fit standard Norton Yokes (the top one being alloy). A Rudge 500cc Ulster engine with four-valve bronze head parts (circa 1934-38), TT Rep profile camshaft, Amal GP carburettor with remote matchbox float, and a Lucas KNR1 racing magneto, powers the NRT. (Courtesy Stewart Wilkins)

NRT Rudge

Stewart Wilkins joined The 59 Club when it moved to Paddington Green in 1964. His ride was a Norton ES2, but he soon progressed onto a Norton Dominator 99 that received the Paul Dunstall treatment. The club house was only 16 miles from his home and one could always open up the throttle on the Western Avenue, A40, which was a dual carriageway. On the ride home after The 59 closed, there was often a visit to the Ace Café, which was only a two mile detour.

Stewart: "I have always been keen on engineering and, along with my first bike, I bought a lathe. I have had at least one motorcycle on the road since passing my motorcycle driving test. Having rebuilt and restored many different machines, I wanted to build something a little different.

"Over the years I had collected a lot of parts, so that in some way dictated the build of the NRT. The name NRT derives from the main components: Norton, Rudge and Triumph, built and owned by myself. I think one the most difficult build problem was making the engine plates, to get everything lined up and the engine as low as possible in the frame. NRT has undergone various upgrades and changes since its inception in the mid '90s, and there are still plans to develop it more.

"NRT is a rider's fun bike; it has not been built to polish and show, although it has been on display and won a few prizes. The brown stains you see on the engine are the remains of 'R' from hard riding. NRT always creates an interest with 'what is it?' being the typical question. It has the legendary Featherbed handling and stops well with the 4LS brake. The engine is very torquey, giving very good acceleration and is currently geared for 100mph @ 5600rpm."

The next special seems to be running an Ulster engine, fitted into a Velocette frame.

Another Rudge Ulster café racer, at the Chalet biker's café in Cowfold, Sussex, March 2009, on the route between Epsom and Brighton. (Courtesy Mark Toynbee)

CHAPTER 5
TRIUMPH

Triumph Engineering Co Ltd started in Coventry in 1885, with production of bicycles, and expanded its operation to include motorcycles from 1898. By the mid-1920s, Triumph had become one of Britain's key motorcycle and car makers. Edward Turner penned the 500cc Speed Twin, introduced in 1937, thus providing the template for all Triumph twins until the 1980s.

After the World War Two blitz of Coventry, production resumed in 1942, but at Meriden in the West Midlands. In 1950, the Thunderbird appeared: basically a 650cc version of the Triumph Speed Twin model. One year later, a race version of the Thunderbird clocked 132mph (212.43km/h) at Utah's Bonneville Salt Flats. In 1959, a tuned twin-carburettor version of the Tiger T110 model, with the T120 designation, was the first Triumph to bear the Bonneville name. The 1960s then saw the BSA Gold Star superseded by the Triton as the iconic café racer special on British roads. Its lively, tunable, mostly Triumph Bonneville-sourced engine, coupled with a Manx Norton chassis, made for a winning combination. As a reminder, some Manx Nortons were bought only for their engines towards the end of the fifties, for use in 500cc Formula 3 car racing, with the rest of the bike being surplus to requirements. This provided a chance for the budding home builder to buy a sharp-handling Featherbed rolling chassis and pair it with an engine from, for example, a crashed Triumph Bonneville and, alas, the Triton was born. This affordable combination also worked well for competitive racing use, as the Methanol-run racing Triton shown below demonstrates.

The T120 Bonneville engine is the most desirable power plant for a Triton, while Norton's Featherbed frames consist of two varieties. The Wideline version, with its parallel top rails and a straight tube from shock absorber to the swingarm pivot, most closely resembles the Manx racers. On the other hand, the Slimline version from the post-1960 period, with its waisted top rails and a curved subframe, is more comfortable for road duty. Triton building peaked in the late 1960s, surely also

The heart of the Speed Twin. (Courtesy Richard Cerrig)

This particular 650 Triton has always been a racing bike and is fitted with a slightly hotter camshaft. The bike was a barn find in New Zealand, rebuilt by Bruce Aitken from the crank up, apart from a friend's help for the setup of the five-speed gearbox and TT carburettors. This Wideline Featherbed Triton competed in several races at the 2015 Burt Munro Challenge racing week, Invercargill, NZ.

helped by Dave Degen's 1965 Barcelona 24-Hours win, on his pre-unit T120 Triton at Montjuic Park, a feat Team Dresda repeated again in 1970. By 1969, Triumph started to struggle against technical progress from Japan, indicating the beginning of the end for the company. John Bloor then revived the famous British marque in the 1980s and set up a new manufacturing plant in Hinckley, Leicestershire in 1988. Production of its modern triple- and four-cylinder models increased from 1992, and by 2000 Triumph was breaking even, and has been a British success story ever since. In 2001, the iconic Bonneville name resurfaced with the release of the eagerly anticipated new 790cc Hinckley parallel-twin, which, although much heavier and not nearly as quick as its predecessor, became an instant hit in its own right. Triumph then released its Thruxton model in 2004, in honour of the '60s café racer cult.

TRIPLE TREAT

Jim Hodges has been riding British motorcycles since the age of 15. He always fancied a Triton and, in 2012, the idea of building a slick ground-up special grew while visiting a pub with a Norvin-owning friend on the Isle of Man. Thereafter, a donor bike in the shape of a 1972 Triumph Trident T150 was sourced privately, and the project was on its way. Jim machined virtually every nut and bolt, stud and spacer for the bike himself. He also made all the alloy engine plates and had them hard anodized, along with brake linkages and footrest brackets. The engine has had just about everything thrown at it, via P&M in Brentford: 10:1 Omega pistons, central plug cylinder head, Megacycle 51135 cams, lightened crank with drilled central oilway, Carrillo con rods, 3x30mm Amal concentric carbs, billet 850cc barrels, hi-flow oil pump, Quaife five-speed close ratio gearbox, Newby

The frame is a 1954 Wideline Featherbed Manx Norton, the short circuit alloy petrol tank was picked up at an auto jumble. The front brake is a magnesium four-leading-shoe Fontana, with alloy rims front and rear. The bike also has racing spec Roadholder forks, connected to the frame with magnesium yokes (triple trees), and sourced from Andy Molnar. The Triton has a magnesium Manx rear wheel, connected to a box section aluminium one-off swingarm. The rear shocks are by Maxton, the steering damper is from Öhlins, and the seat unit is alloy, made by Neil Adams from Made in Metal. (Courtesy Jim Hodges/Neil Adams)

dry clutch and belt drive, and Pazon electronic ignition. Mal, from Metal Malarkey, built the exhausts, and the end cones with baffles attached were Jim's handiwork. The bike weighs in at a wet 185kg and produces an estimated 85hp, with a top speed of 130mph. This immaculate build took around eight months from start to finish, which included buying the donor Trident and Norton parts. The reason Jim remembers this well is because it took this long to wait for the front wheel of his bike!

TriBSA

Steve Clark built the below TriBSA special (called The Bitch) in 1968, using a BSA frame, Norton Roadholder forks, and a tuned 750cc Triumph Thunderbird engine. He always considered a BSA frame a better choice over a Norton chassis, hence going down the more

The TriBSA on display at the Brackley Bike Festival, 2014. (Courtesy Trevor Earl)

Steve's bike in the Festival of Jurby pit lane in 2015.

This nice TriBSA attended the 2015 VMCC Manx Rally Regularity Run. Right: Closeup of fuel tank and engine.

unusual 'bitsa' café racer route. The engine consists of a Mk1 Morgo 750cc cylinder barrel mated to gas-flowed T140 heads, and equipped with Amal GP carburettors. A lightened crank and BSA Gold Star RRT2 gearbox complement the package. In charge of scrubbing off speed at the front is a 260mm Fontana four-leading-shoe drum brake, the rear is an original BSA item. The oil tank stems from a BSA Gold Star.

Next is a nice TriBSA parked at a classics gathering in Tynwald, Isle of Man

Triumph Legend

Former Triumph racing manager Les Williams developed the 964cc British special motorcycle, on the opposite page, after the collapse of the Triumph Meriden plant, from parts specific to customer requirements. The bikes were based on the Triumph T160V Trident three-cylinder motor, carefully tuned for maximum performance, and equipped with a five-speed gearbox and electric start. A Lockheed hydraulic system, with twin discs at the front and single rear, improved braking performance. Les built a total of sixty Triumph Legends between 1984 and 1992.

Triumph / Spondon

Neil Kiddie owns the fine racer below, built in 1990. The engine stems from a 1961-built 500cc two-cylinder OHV T100 Triumph,

The Triumph Legend 964cc triple in British Racing Green livery, basking in the Jurby carpark.

fitted into a 1972 Spondon frame. This bike also has an MOT for daytime road use. The T100 Tiger series launched in 1939 and was capable of 100mph (160km/h); it was a success from the outset, which in turn translated to excellent revenue for the Triumph factory. The T100 then appeared in 1954, fitted with a cast iron cylinder block and head, soon replaced with a light alloy head with special airways to improve cooling.

Bob Stevenson and Stuart Tiller started their motorcycle frame business in 1969, in the village of Spondon, Derbyshire. They initially wanted to improve club racing BSA Gold Stars with their own frame design, but had their breakthrough when working on a custom chassis with a Greeves engine. One success story involved building custom frames for Yamahas in the early '70s, culminating in the 1982 British 250cc GP Championship win by Germany's Martin Wimmer on a Spondon-framed Yamaha. Alongside road racing, the company was also manufacturing frames for a variety of road bike engines. Spondon later became involved in the Norton rotary project, supplying the lightweight beam-section frame for the F1.

The Spondon-framed Triumph on display in Tynwald.

The engine stems from a 750cc T140 Triumph Bonneville, fitted with 2x30mm Amal carburettors. The frame is a YSC item, with a rake of 28 degrees. The front end is from Triumph, the swingarm made, again, by YSC. (Courtesy Yuri Shif Custom)

The café racer runs on 16in H-D wheels, and is fitted with Shinko 3.0-16 tyres. Yuri's inhouse paint job is termed Gipsy Racing Green. Other YSC fabricated parts are the exhaust, gas tank, handlebars, seat, foot controls, and instruments. (Courtesy Yuri Shif Custom)

Yuri Shif Custom (YSC)

The popularity of café racers is truly an international phenomenon, only initially confined to the British Isles. Yuri Shif is an accomplished bike builder from Minsk, Belarus. He built this Bonneville-based special in 2011, to satisfy his customer Kostyan's café racer aspirations.

UNITY TRITON

Unity (Equipe) Spares Ltd, in Staveley, Chesterfield, specialises in Manx Norton, Triumph, and Triton motorcycles. Following an arrangement with John Tickle (the then holder of the Manx name), dating back to 1978, the company has since held the sole rights to the use of the name 'Manx' as a motorcycle type, together with the rights to produce new spares – and even complete machines – of the respected Manx design. Its range of products now also includes Unity Manx Triton frames for the Hinckley Bonneville range.

TRIUMPH METISSE

Derek and Don Rickman's motorcycle business initially started with modifying scramblers in the '50s, and later progressed to producing its own Metisse labelled scrambler frames. Its chassis design accommodated every British twin engine with the appropriate engine plates. In 1966 the company offered privateer road racers and regular road rider Tarmac versions of its Metisse frames.

The company also produced road bikes, initially using a Triumph Bonneville engine. Rickman's road bikes were the first to use disc brakes front and rear: a joint project with Lockheed. The company's other inventions include the use of large diameter telescopic forks of up to 40mm, in conjunction with Spanish firm Betor, and oil carried

Above: A Unity Triton parked close to the Douglas Grandstand: note its swept-back exhaust.

A Triumph Metisse with high pipes, on the Isle of Man.

Godden's 1000cc SOHC V-Twin was initially intended for grass-track sidecar racing. The 1000cc V-twin engine was produced by former European Grasstrack Champion Don Godden, and is good for 128hp when running on Methanol, but, in this application, is tuned back to 100hp for everyday road use. (Courtesy Yesterday's NL)

Front view of the nickel-plated Metisse frame.

in the frame tubes to reduce weight and help dissipate heat. In the late '60s Rickman commissioned Harry Weslake to develop a 749cc eight-valve cylinder head conversion for Triumph 650cc twins, which in turn lead to a twenty per cent performance increase over standard figures. In the '80s Rickmans sold a portion of their business to concentrate on kit cars. Several niche companies still produce versions of the Metisse frames today.

GODDEN CAFÉ RACER

The Rickman Metisse frame was suitable for all sorts of motors, and could even be found with engines such as this rare Godden V-twin Special.

HYDE HARRIER

Norman Hyde worked for Triumph as an apprentice in 1964 and has been involved with the marque ever since. Following the Meriden factory closure in 1973, he set up shop in early 1976, designing and selling performance parts for Triumph twins and triples. Norman was well qualified for his new venture, having worked in Triumph's

A 930cc 1975 Triumph Hyde Harrier, owned by Kenneth R Drysdale, in the Jurby pit area. .

racing development department under Doug Hele. Hyde was directly involved in the development of the T120 to T180 models, as well as projects that never made it into production. In 1987, his firm introduced the Hyde Harrier, a café racer kit for Triumph Bonneville and Trident engines, using a frame developed in conjunction with Harris Performance. Naturally, the company offers performance and styling parts for John Bloor's Hinckley Bonnevilles, as well as to recreate the classic feel of the Sixties.

In November 2013, following a couple of trips to the Beezumph rally in England, Jeff Elliott thought it would be a good idea to build a triple. He purchased a frame kit from Norman Hyde (the bike is based on a Hyde Harrier), but the kit sat in his friend's garage for best part of a year, while he collected more bits and worked on a Seeley café racer project.

The engine he ended up with came from several sources, but the crankcases came from a guy called Tony Osbourn, who raced Rob Norths in the '70s. The barrels are Nova classics, with 850cc

Above: Jeff Elliot's triple. The front yokes, footrests, 3-into-1 exhaust, brake caliper bracket, head steady inlet, manifolds, coil brackets, and fairing brackets are all home-built. The front forks are from a Yamaha R6, basically Öhlins, too. Brakes are R6 radial Gold Spots onto 310mm Fireblade discs. The carriers that fit the discs to the wheels are homemade.

Omega forged pistons running on steel Arrow con rods. The crank was balanced at Basset Down Balancing, and the head has hard seats and P&M valves. The Carburettors are 28mm Keihin flat slides with the cams re-profiled to half race spec. The clutch is a Triples Rule aluminium unit from the States, running to an LP Williams belt drive. The electric start is a Madigan unit, also from the United States. Sparks are taken care of by a tri-spark unit from NZ, and the gearbox is currently standard. Jeff had the frame nickel plated and bought a set of new Astralite wheels to go with it. The rear suspension is fitted with an Öhlins remote reservoir.

Left: Dave Mead's Classic and Hinckley Tritons. Right: Triton on a toy run. It consists of a '59 Wideline and later pre-unit 750 Morgo top end, gearbox converted to five-speed, Triumph conical rear hub, and front drum brake upgraded to twin disc Bonneville unit for added safety, plus 'bacon slicer' front brake cooling rings and trademark swept-back exhausts. Centre: The man himself. (Courtesy Dave Mead)

CLASSIC & HINCKLEY TRITONS

Dave Mead has been into bikes as long as he can remember. His dad had a solo bike and an Ariel 600 side-valve sidecar as family transport, and later used a BSA Bantam to commute in and out of Birmingham. Dave's mum hailed from London, a stone's throw from the Ace Café. She was already married with kids when her younger brothers and sisters were rockers. Dave's uncle Jim called in regularly on his Triton outfit in the mid-60s, when Dave was a young lad, so the seed was planted. Dave started out with a BSA A10-powered mongrel sidecar, which soon lost its chair for solo use. In 1979 he came across an all red-painted 1959 Triton, lingering in a modern bike shop. The bike was subsequently bought, stripped, and rebuilt to resemble his uncle's Triton.

All of Dave's mates had T140 Bonnies, and he reckons he only beat them racing because he had no brakes. He was doing the rocker thing in the late '70s to early '80s, when it was mostly all about heavy rock, but some of them would also seek out rock-'n'-roll dos. Eventually, Dave entered the racing scene from 1989 to 2000, where he won two classic championships on a Slippery Sam replica. He also raced in three Manx Grand Prix events, and spent ten years Hare and Hounds Enduro racing, including three Weston Beach races.

Dave built his Hinckley Triton in the winter of 1999, consisting of a '59 Wideline frame, '93 Tiger 900 triple engine, swingarm, and rear wheel, a '70s twin-disc Meriden front end, and done-up as the original Slippery Sam. He describes his build as a wolf in sheep's clothing, and great for chasing after modern machines.

CHRIS SPAETT TRITON

Chris Spaett rebuilt the below Triton a long time ago. The bike consists of a nickel plated Wideline Featherbed frame, with a late unit 650cc engine built to Bonneville specs, Norton Roadholder forks with Norton wheels and brakes, and alloy tanks. The aim when building it was

Over 10,000 miles after its rebuild, it's still oil-tight and goes really well, running on Castrol R for all of that time. (www.ventureclassics.co.uk)

Chris' Triton has gained a few battle scars and a pair of 'bacon slicers' along the way. (www.ventureclassics.co.uk)

Far right: Another Hinckley Triton on the Festival of Jurby carpark, Very much in the same vein as Dave's bike. (Owner unknown).

to have nothing painted, but it has gained a couple of painted parts over the years. It has been a Triton since the 1960s. Chris much regretted the selling of this bike; he sold it in 2003 to free up funds to set up his motorcycle shop, Venture Classics, in the Herefordshire countryside. To his amazement, the Triton resurfaced on eBay in the summer of 2006, so he was able to buy it back from the buyer he originally sold it to. Much to his delight, the Triton was in the same condition as it was when he sold it three years earlier, apart from a couple of minor faults that it had developed. The worst of them was a big oil leak, which turned out to be nothing more than the drain plug on the primary case having fallen out.

TONY FOALE TRIUMPH

Tony Foale has been into motorcycles since his mid teens, be it road riding or bike racing. He holds an impressive engineering background, which led him to work in areas such as mathematics, computer science, car manufacturing, nuclear science, and ultimately motorcycle chassis design. Educated in Australia, he moved to England in 1971 to reside closer to the Isle of Man racing action. In 1973 he turned his passion into a business making frame kits for racing bikes. Many of these machines were highly successful, and included championship winning sidecars. From the early '80s, Tony embarked on improving front suspension systems and steering geometry for motorcycles, which led to

Tony made only a few Trident frames, which were basically like the Kawa/Honda/Suzy frames that he made many more of. (Courtesy Toney Foale)

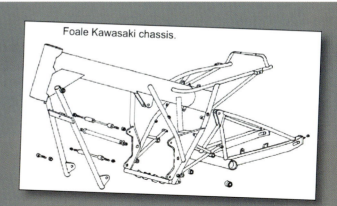

The Trident frame is estimated to have been built between 1976 and the early 1980s. The rear engine mounting, front downtubes, and electrics brackets would have been the main changes on the Trident frame, compared to the Kawasaki frame example shown. (Courtesy Tony Foale)

the publication of several books on motorcycle handling and chassis design. He now lives in Spain and acts as a consultant on various vehicular projects. Right is an example of a Tony Foale-framed Triumph Triple.

Tri2Ton

Peter Andrews has been building Café Racers and Specials since the age of 16, and is the builder of the Tri2Ton, the twin engined Triton right.

He had been thinking about this project for 40 years when, in 2009, his eyes lit at an autojumble: he spotted a dealer selling an ex-Norton wide line frame that had been extended 6in for drag racing, complete with short Roadholder forks and swinging arm. Peter already had engine parts for two complete 650 Bonneville motors and a couple of AMC gearboxes, so he could now start working on his dream. First he had to decide which configuration to have with the engines, so after making different plywood engine plates, he decided on the V-type design, making alloy engine plates to suit. Unfortunately, the gearbox would not go into place correctly, requiring the machining of the inner case, in order for it to fit.

Once the drivetrain was lined up perfectly, he fabricated an oil tank template out of cardboard, big enough to hold 16 pints of oil, which Exactweld made for him in alloy, with two outlets and two

The Tri2Ton won the Classic Bike of the Year title in 2010. (Courtesy Mick Barton)

The Tri2Ton is the only registered road-legal twin engine 1300cc Triton in England. (Courtesy Peter Andrews)

inlets to supply each engine separately. The front forks were uprated with sidecar springs, and the rear suspension received stainless rear shocks from Hagon, with 26kg springs. Peter then bought new front and rear Akront alloy rims and tyres, fitted with a Triumph conical rear hub and a Suzuki 4 Leader for the front. The Lucerne green and GM silver paint job was chosen by his wife Pat. With the engines now rebuilt to Bonnie specs, the awkward part of connecting them up came next. Peter got in touch with John Newby, to make him a complete belt drive system, linking the engines and his racing clutch, which all came back perfectly. Sadly, the standard alternator didn't work, so he looked around until he came up with a small Kuboto belt drive system of an American digger, which he used to tension the engine pulleys. The petrol tank consists of a short alloy circuit type. With it all together, he tried to start it, but it had too much compression and would not kick over. Peter then came up with the idea of some cable operated-type decompression valves, with a 14mm thread, and off came the front cylinder head ... then central plug inserts put in, before refitting it all back together. He then tried again, pulling in the decompression valves and – hey presto – it kicked over and started the rear engine. So he slowly shut the valves, it pulled in the back engine, and started brilliantly.

CRK CAFÉ RACER KITS

CRK's Ian Saxcoburg is a mechanical design engineer from the Isle of Wight, who started building café racer kits for older Hondas, first unveiled at the Bristol Classic Show in 2013. His kits can be bought as modules, as one progresses a build, or as a complete kit to transform one's bike at home. The enthusiastic response to his work encouraged him to develop a further kit, designed for Triumph Triples, with the prototype, shown below, completed in February 2015. The kit is designed to fit the Sprint, Trident, Daytona, Trophy, and Speed Triple models, which have the T300 engine with carburettors and spine frame, manufactured from 1992-1996. It's very nice work indeed.

Above and right: This sleek machine started life as a 1996 Sprint Executive tourer. The nice bodywork and Hurricane orange and yellow paint job really transformed the Hinckley triple. (Courtesy Café Racer Kits)

JEROLAMO

Mr Martini is a well-known customiser from Verona, Italy, and has been modifying Triumph's for some time. For the custom shown below – named Jerolamo – Nicola Martini used a year-2000 Triumph Legend TT as a donor bike. First he changed the front axle for a Ducati item, fitted upside down Showa front forks, a Brembo front wheel disc, half handlebars, and alloy rims to the old girl. Next, he redesigned the rear of the bike to raise the riding position, along with raising the fuel tank, under which he relocated the electrics. The handmade seat, supported by a chrome frame, received a bordeaux coloured cover with cream piping. The glossy black contrasts well with the chromed 3-into-1 Zard exhaust. The bike was initially fitted with a classic looking endurance style windscreen, but Nicola liked the naked look better in the end.

The 885cc Custom Triple was the winner of the Motor Bike Expo 2013. (Courtesy Mr Martini)

The 885cc 70hp Triumph Legend TT is one of the best incarnations of the original big Hinckley triples, and should provide plenty of fun in its new clothes. (Courtesy Mr Martini)

JEROLAMO 675R

Nicola Martini didn't shy away from giving Triumph's Daytona 675R a set of new clothes, either. The donor bike for the following custom creation stems from 2011, and is claimed to develop 130hp for the 180kg café racer triple.

An upside-down Öhlins unit takes care of the front suspension, while a Showa damper takes care of the rear. Front brakes are from Brembo and rear brakes are from Nissin, while tyres are Metzeler Racetec Interact 120/70-17 at the front, Metzeler Interact 180/55-17 at the rear.

The Jerolamo R is fitted with Kineo rims, a handmade chromed steel rear subframe, and a café racer screen with a Triumph America headlight. The lovely 3-into-1 exhaust is sourced from Zard, the seat is handmade, and the rear light is a CEV item. (Courtesy Mr Martini)

WESLAKE

Olivi Motori is yet another outfit from Italy, to be exact, a Triumph dealership based in Florence. Vittorio describes his build as an exercise in passion, and named it Weslake as a tribute to multitalented tuning specialist Harry Weslake, who was well known in the Triton fraternity for his eight-valve cylinder heads. This very modern looking café racer is based on a T509 Speed Triple, with most components hailing from Triumph's own parts bin, like the modified Thruxton tail unit and the Speed Triple 1050 derived rear wheel. Instrumentation is taken care of by a Motoscope unit from Motogadget, the triple clamps are

The 108hp aluminium-framed custom is a former prizewinner in the Best Naked Class of the Verona Motor Bike Expo. (Courtesy Olivi Motori)

The Weslake is a job well done. The Speed Triple had its bug eye headlamps replaced in favour of a single light unit around a bikini fairing. (Courtesy Olivi Motori)

from Robbymoto, and the front rim stems from Marchesini. The biggest job was to reduce and hide the electrical system, for which Vittorio built a tub which perfectly emulates the frame, in the airbox compartment, to accommodate the entire electrical installation, along with deletion of the airbox in favour of cone filters. The whole build is yet another good example of what can be done with Hinckley triples.

THUNDERBIRD SPORT

MCN UK rated Triumph's Thunderbird Sport a surprisingly cool, versatile and fun retro package. This sportier Hinckley model received revised styling to mimic the 1971 X75 Hurricane, with its 3-into-2 exhausts and cheese grater air filter covers. It was built from 1997 to 2003, and has developed into a bit of a cult object amidst the Triumph carburettor models, as well as being relatively rare. It also lends itself to a spot of customisation, as shown below.

The 885cc wire-wheeled, twin disc, year 2000 triple, with its Opal White and Tangerine Orange paint scheme, looks good with the aftermarket reverse cone silencers fitted. The humped seat and cockpit fairing finish off the package.

HINCKLEY THRUXTON BONNEVILLE

Triumph's headquarters had contemplated the Thruxton Bonneville concept since 1996, with the project getting under way in July 2001. The café racer was finally launched in November 2003, for the 2004 model year, as the sports bike of the range and to celebrate the famous race bikes of the '60s; in particular, the Thruxton 500 endurance event, in Hampshire, an event for production-based road machines which saw Triumph take the top three podium positions in 1969.

Larger pistons gave the new Thruxton engine an 865cc displacement over the standard 790cc 62hp Bonneville, alongside new camshafts and re-jetted carburettors. These measures resulted in 69hp and a livelier performance over the base Bonneville, nicely matched with a fruitier exhaust note from the re-worked pipes. Lastly, a steeper steering angle, upgraded forks, longer rear suspension, and improved brakes completed the new package.

This Triumph T120 Thruxton Replica gives a taste of the modern Thruxton Bonnie's ancestry. (www.ventureclassics.co.uk)

A fly screen, drop handlebars, rear-set foot pegs, upswept exhaust, and humped seat complete the café racer visuals. (Courtesy Triumph)

The Thruxton is aimed at riders who like the style and heritage of the café era, but with modern engineering. (Courtesy Triumph)

Thruxton Ace

Triumph released the Thruxton Ace Special Edition model in 2015, to celebrate the company's association with the legendary Ace Café in north London. The historic connection with the '60s biker hangout was envisioned through a white paintjob, contrasted with the bike's black painted engine, an oxblood coloured custom seat, detachable colour matched seat hump, Ace Café logos on the side panels, fuel tank, and tail unit, proper bar-end mirrors, and a special handlebar plaque.

Continued on page 89

The Thruxton Ace sports a nice profile. (Courtesy Triumph)

The 865cc parallel-twin, with its low-slung handlebar and wire-spoke aluminium wheels, is a current and reliable retro version of the home-built road burners of yore. (Courtesy Triumph)

The Thruxton on café racer home turf.
(Courtesy Triumph)

The paintjob emphasizes the long and low appearance.

An unknown rider in period dress, about to head off from Ramsay.

It's no secret that Triumph's Hinckley twins are a popular base for café customisation, amidst a healthy aftermarket support network for the Bonneville range of bikes. Opposite are some examples.

JB Thruxton

John Blair: "The bike below belonged to my son Jonny, who died four years ago. He had started the café racer project, but never got to see it finished. I found his drawings and plans and decided to finish the job to his specifications, as a living memory, and I love my trips to the Isle of Man on it.

"It officially belongs now to my grandson Jonny Jun, but he is only five years old, so I will have it for a while yet, thank God! Bruce Anstey had his photo taken on it at the 2014 Manx GP and had to get it running to hear the sound of it."

Jonny's café racer started life as a 2006 standard Thruxton. Changes to date have been an upgrade to a Norman Hyde big bore kit (re-jetted to suit the engine tweaks), the AI unit removed, Hagon rear shocks and matching progressive front springs fitted, Triumph off-road loud pipes, and an 18-tooth front sprocket. Further mods are both front and rear mudguards replaced in alloy, side casings removed and replaced with alloy number plates, and also the chain guard and front sprocket housing receiving the same treatment. Lastly, the graphics were designed by Jonny and reproduced by Sign It in Northern Ireland.

The fuel tank has been styled on a five-gallon Manx Norton.

Jim runs the bike on super unleaded fuel, with 5ml of Castrol R per gallon, so it looks good, sounds good, and smells good. Tab 2 Classics, in Wales, made a Ducati Imola-type seat for Jim, finished in black suede. It also made a false fixing strap for the tank to add to the classic look.

WATER-COOLED BONNIE 900

Come 2016, and Triumph has gone the whole hog in reinventing its Bonneville range, after four years of development. The first of two new engine platforms translates into the 900cc Street Twin model below. The new liquid-cooled eight-valve parallel-twin, with 270 degree firing order, is equipped with ride-by-wire fuel-injection and engine management, which in turn equates to 18 per cent more torque and 36 per cent better fuel economy than its predecessor. Further news items are the brushed stainless steel exhaust system, greater suspension travel, and a lower seat with better seat foam.

The new 900cc Street Twin is available in five different colour schemes. (Courtesy Triumph)

The Street Twin is the base model, ready for customisation, with Triumph components, or predesigned Scrambler, Brat Tracker, or Urban Style inspiration kits on offer. (Courtesy Triumph)

Engine side cover still life. (Courtesy Triumph)

BONNEVILLE 1200 T120

Triumph continues to play its heritage card with the new T120 Bonneville variants, the bike's styling inspired by the marque's 1959 Bonneville ancestor. The new models are available in two-tone paint, or black and/or Matt Graphite livery, respectively, and fitted with Triumph's new water-cooled 1200cc parallel-twin engine. The new eight-valve parallel-twin motor, also with a 270 degree firing order (as with Triumph's new 900cc unit), has 54 per cent more peak torque than its Bonneville predecessor. The engine's retro look is retained with cooling fins and mock carburettors.

The T120 received an all-new chassis and suspension, along with ride-by-wire fuel-injection, an engine management system, ABS, and traction control. (Courtesy Triumph)

Thruxton 1200 Bonneville

The also new-for-2016 1200cc Triumph Thruxton Bonneville, is the ultimate modern classic café racer, and has lifted the Thruxton name to a new level over its 865cc predecessor. Peak torque of this parallel-twin engine is up 62 per cent over its previous generation model. Three ride-by-wire modes assist its lively performance, backed up again by engine management, ABS, and traction control. Triumph really went all-out to capture a much bigger slice of the burgeoning custom market with the release of this sports classic model. To top the balance sheet, just one more extra bit; the 'R' designated sister model is kitted-out with Showa Big Piston forks, Öhlins rear suspension, twin floating Brembo disks and monobloc callipers, and Pirelli Diablo Rosso Corsa Tyres.

Classic style bar-end mirrors look the business. (Courtesy Triumph)

The 1200cc factory café racer took its inspiration from the original Bonneville Thruxton. (Courtesy Triumph)

Loads of accessories, such as this cockpit fairing, are on offer for personalisation of the new model. (Courtesy Triumph)

The Thruxton 1200 R is painted in either Diablo Red or Silver Ice livery. (Courtesy Triumph)

CHAPTER 6
VELOCETTE TO WESLAKE

Veloce Ltd was founded in 1905 in Birmingham, and run by the Goodman family. Their venture produced quality hand-built motorcycles in small numbers. Racing success sells, and the company engaged in competitions as early as 1920, right through to the 1950s, claiming the 1949 and 1950 World Championship in the 350cc class in the process.

The firm's first two-stroke offering, in 1913, was named Velocette, and the name was kept for subsequent models. In 1925, Veloce introduced the overhead camshaft four-stroke 350cc K series. From 1926, the company entered uprated K models in Isle of Man TT races with great success, resulting in the launch of the KTT production racing model, produced from 1928 to 1949.

The 250cc MOV was introduced in 1933 as the first of a new line of more affordable overhead valve motorcycles, a popular bike capable of 78mph (126km/h), and the ancestor of all the pushrod singles.

David Bardwell's Velocette KTT racer on the IoM.

Velocette MOV 250 Special (rider Des Evens), in Jurby.

Lengthening the stroke of the MOV crankshaft spawned the MAC 350cc in 1934, which became another successful model. The 500cc MSS saw the light in 1935, a touring mount suitable for sidecar use, fitted with a new frame derived from the KTT racing bike. In 1954, the MSS found favour in North American desert racing circles, leading to the inception of Scrambler and Enduro versions of the bike, namely the 349cc Viper and 499cc Venom. The Viper was no slouch, with Eddie Dow doing well over 100mph on a Clubman equipped Viper at the 1957 Thruxton race. The same goes for the Venom, when in 1961 a production Venom broke a memorable world record, in holding an average speed of 100.05mph (161km/h) over a 24-hour period. With a world record pedigree, it's not surprising that the Charles Udall designed Venom ended up becoming the bestseller of the Velocette model range.

The nice Venom hybrid below was spotted in the 2015 Jurby event pit lane.

A nice Venom MK2 Clubman, parked near the Douglas Grandstand, with closeup of Ace bars ... make it in any colour as long as it's black!

This nicely executed hybrid Norton Venom drew plenty of attention.

BSA Gold Star production ended in 1963, and an opportunity beckoned for Veloce. This was tasked to Bertie Goodman, who fitted a racing cylinder head to the Venom allowing the use of extra-large valves and a downdraught inlet port, thus effectively creating the Velocette Thruxton. The Venom Thruxton was first shown at the 1964 Earls Court Show, and aimed straight at the gap which the BSA Gold Star's demise had left in the marketplace. Although the Thruxton was sold as a road bike, it was really aimed at the racing community. The machine had a respectable weight of 170kg and produced 41hp @ 6200rpm, with a compression ratio of 9.0:1, good for a top speed of 115mph (185km/h). An impact on the race scene followed quickly: Dave Dixon and Joe Dunphy won the 1965 Thruxton 500 event at Castle Combe on a Velocette Thruxton, and Neil Kelly and Keith Heckles achieved first and second podiums in the 1967 Production TT. Despite the success of the Thruxton, Veloce was struggling, and the late sixties heralded the end of production for Velocette motorcycles. Finally, in February 1971 the company closed its doors for good.

Velocette Racing New Zealand (VRNZ) is a bunch of like-minded, but differently skilled individuals, amongst them Phil Price, the owner of the two racing specials below, with an interesting story attached to them.

ELDEE 2

The Eldee Velocette was the creation of South Australian Les Diener, a major racing competitor on the Australian stage from the end of World War Two until the mid-50s, on a highly modified, alcohol fuelled, prewar rigid frame 1935 Velocette 250cc MOV. He even defeated works Guzzi rider Fergus Anderson during an Australia tour in 1949, at Woodside. In 1953, Les decided to lift his game to become even more competitive in designing a double overhead camshaft top end, using the pushrod MOV engine as the basis for his Eldee special (named after his initials, LD). He fabricated the patterns for the cylinder head and rocker box himself, while retaining the original 68x68mm bore x stroke of the bike. The new motor was fitted with a four-speed close-ratio Velocette gearbox, and housed in a Manx Norton inspired duplex cradle frame finished off with shortened BSA C10 forks, BSA wheels, and a streamlined seat and tail fairing. In 1956, Diener won the Australian TT, at Mildura, on the Eldee, timed at a respectable 116mph (186.6km/h), this time fitted with a dustbin fairing. After a major crash in 1957, Diener loaned the Eldee to Ken Rumble until 1961, before the bike was sold to pursue

A Velocette Thruxton 500cc four-stroke single on display. The Thruxton's single Amal carburettor was so big a special cutout at the back of the fuel tank to accommodate it was required. (Courtesy Ron Saunders)

The Eldee 2 in the pit lane at the 2015 Burt Munro Challenge street races, Invercargill, NZ.

The Eldee 2 sports a modified Norton International frame, with a Norton fork at the front and Koni items at the rear. Above: A peek at the cylinder head.

Below: The Big Velo's 500cc engine produces 38hp @ 6000rpm and sits in a rigid frame, guided by Webb-built works girder forks at the front, and single-leading-shoe brakes fitted front and rear.

other interests. In 1983, Les successfully entered the fray again, on yet another Velocette MOV racer. But it wasn't until a 1987 invitation to a New Zealand Classic Racing Register meeting, that he was inspired to source many of the patterns from the original Eldee to produce a replica of his DOHC Velocette special, the Eldee 2, pictured above. Current New Zealand custodian Phil Price, mechanic Nick Thomson, and rider Chris Swallow keep this outstanding piece of Australian racing history alive. They started racing the rejuvenated Eldee 2 from 2012 onwards, and have won two NZCMRR 250cc titles to date in the process.

THE BIG VELO

The Big Velo is an affectionate term for one special motorcycle, which entered NZ's shores in 1934 ... but not before it won the Ulster Grand Prix under Walter Rusk in the same year. Code named MT5001, the Big Velo was built by Veloce as an experimental factory racer, developed from the 350cc K series and enlarged in displacement in order to compete in the 500cc 'Blue Riband' class. Veloce considered local

From left: Rear view of the custom-made seat and alloy fuel tank. The engine has Velocette Viper crankcases (the original Venom versions were a bit of a mess, and the Viper ones are the same, engine numbers aside). It's still a 500cc, with a dynamically balanced crank, Alpha big end, 8.75:1 compression ratio, and Alfin barrel.

dealer William White a worthy recipient to race MT5001 in colonial New Zealand to propound the marque's glory, and it sure did. MT5001 became New Zealand's most successful racing motorcycle between 1935 and 1966, winning no fewer than eight national titles, five national beach championships, and eight NZ TTs, most notably under rider Len Perry. But the Big Velo is far from retirement and still on active duty, with Phil Price still engaging riders such as Chris Swallow and Bill Biber to let Big Velo loose in numerous New Zealand Classic Racing events.

THE VELTON

Malcolm Sanger's 'Velton' special started life back in the late sixties as a union of Norton and Velocette Venom parts for a race bike project. It had a Thruxtonised motor and a Wideline Featherbed frame, and was bought by a now departed dear friend of his in an unfinished state. The said friend turned it into a basic version of what it is now, but in an 'oily rag' trim. Malcolm bought the bike from his friend's widow, and it stood in his workshop for eight years until he finally decided to restore it into a 21st century café racer. Malcolm: It was quite a job, but it left me with a bike that handles beautifully, goes really well, looks fabulous, but most of all, gives me a huge grin factor that I couldn't buy anywhere, and I can at least say 'I med it meself.'

The Velton's clock pods are Triumph T150 items, grafted onto a Norton top yoke, with original speedo and rev counter. The handlebar switches and levers are Honda. The oil tank is homemade, along

with the other alloy parts. Malcolm's mate 'Big Al' custom-made the wiring loom, and the BTH self-generating Mag now runs a twin-plug head. A lightweight lithium ion battery feeds the Alton electric starter and 12V alternator. The carburretion is taken care of by a 32mm Mk2 Concentric carb, with home brewed bell-mouth. Further items are a Kevin Thurston belt drive clutch with, Yamaha R1 plates and crank oil seal, and a Velocette gearbox with TT close ratio gear set. Most stainless fasteners, and everything else from back to front, were made in Malc's workshop. His biggest headache was the sprocket alignment: let's just say it's very close. Oh, and not to forget the gate valve steering damper given to him by a friend as a joke!

Malcolm's love affair with motorcycles started at the age of 12 and has never left him. His first real bike was a Norton Model 50 in 1965, but when the engine expired, his café racer days started. Out came the motor and in went a Triumph T100 SS, along with alloy guards, clip-ons, fibreglass tank, megaphones, and anything else he could get his hands on. Malcolm stems from the Black Country, an area of the West Midlands in England which he termed an "engineer's paradise" in the old days. He started work as a bike mechanic at the age of 15, in 1964, which was apparently a great job with rubbish wages. In 1965 he slowly moved into car body repairs, and later into the industrial side of painting car parts for manufacturers like Aston Martin, Ferrari, et al. When semi-retired, he created a 900sq ft workshop with a lathe, miller, welder, spray booth, and all of the other tools a bloke needs to help make his dreams come true.

VINCENT

Phil Vincent acquired the trademark and remaining stock of HRD Motors Ltd in 1928, soon renaming the venture Vincent HRD Co Ltd, with production moving to Stevenage. The HRD name was finally dropped and superseded by the Vincent designation in 1949. Gifted engineer Phil Irving joined Vincent in 1931 and, by 1934, penned the OHV 500cc Meteor single. Next, he designed the revered V-twin engine, which gave birth to the Vincent HRD Series A Rapide, introduced in late 1936. The following year, Irving decided to team up with Velocette, but re-joined Vincent in 1943. The Series B Rapide model (designed during the war and introduced before the end of hostilities) differed from the A model, in that the cylinder angle was now 50 degrees instead of the 47.5 degrees previously. This, amongst other changes, permitted the use of the engine as a stressed member of the frame.

The 1948 Series C Rapide was distinguished from the Series B version by its Girder forks with hydraulic damping. By 1950, the Rapide/Black Shadow produced between 45-55hp respectively, with the Black Shadow being capable of 125mph. The Black Lightning racer was substantially lightened by replacing many steel parts with aluminium, and gathered many speed records in the early '50s. Apart from the 500cc Meteor single, the company also built the 500cc Comet and 500cc Grey Flash racer. In the 1930s, Vincent took its 500cc model to the Senior TT and engaged a works Series A Rapide in short circuit meetings.

Factory participation in postwar racing was only burning on a small flame, which can't be said of the many privateers, who more than made up for the factory's lack of racing engagement, be this in the past, or even up to the present day. In 1955, Invercargill-born New Zealander Russell Wright raised the solo world's maximum speed record to 185.15mph (298km/h) with a privately owned Vincent Black Lightning, alongside Bob Burns who achieved 162mph (260.71km/h) on the Vincent with a third wheel fitted, on the same day. It's also noteworthy that Vincent-HRD dealer Jack Surtees obtained, during one of his factory visits, a dismantled 500cc Grey Flash racer, which he modified to nurture his son's racing talent, future World Champion John Surtees. John promptly won the June 1951 Brands Hatch 500cc and 1000cc races, and continued to ride the Vincent-HRD on a winning streak until August 1952, before changing over to a

The Egli Vincent Grey Flash racer produces 60hp, with a 92.02x75.20mm bore x stroke. (Courtesy Cedric Janodet)

Featherbed Norton Manx. In 1949, Vincent's George and Cliff Brown had hands-on involvement in the development of the 500cc Grey Flash racing project, which was later promoted as a racer, despite the company downplaying its wares for anything other than road use at any other time. Competitive on short circuits, the racing engine produced 35hp @ 6200rpm, with a compression ratio of 8:1, and fitted with an Amal 32mm TT carburettor, Albion gearbox, and weighing a mere 330lb (150kg). Vincent managed to squeeze yet another 10mph (16km/h) out of a more modified, higher revving Grey Flash to compete in the 1950s Senior TT.

GODET VINCENT 500CC RACER

Frenchman Patrick Godet has had a love affair with Vincent motorcycles longer than most, in fact he has been working on Vincents for 40 years, and raced them successfully from 1979 to 1983. His Normandy-based business initially only restored bikes, whereas he now also produces small volumes of Black Lightning Vincents with the Egli style frame. The legacy of the fabulous Egli Vincent is kept alive, and the bike is fully endorsed by its original creator, Fritz Egli, to the point that Egli gave Godet the rights to use the name Egli on his Vincent engined racing machines. Patrick works on his engines

Opposite page and above: The Grey Flash Godet bike. (Courtesy Sandra Gillard)

and components mostly in house, so as not to compromise his high standards of quality. In 2014, he finished an Egli Vincent Grey Flash 500 single-cylinder racer in the vein of John Surtees's bike, which had its first outing at the IoM Classic TT in the same year. Godet's rider, Bruno Leroy, ended the bike's first race due to a loose exhaust, but it won't be long before the Vincent single gives bikes such as the Norton Manx or Matchless G50 a run for their money.

The Godet single racer's technical specs amount to: a one piece crankshaft, plain bearing titanium conrod, Omega piston, one piece aluminium coated French-made cylinder, stainless steel valves, Beryllium seats, a modern oil pump, British cast magnesium crankcases and gearbox shells, a non-self-generating electronic ignition with lithium battery, a 40mm Gardner carb, oil filters on both feed and return, a NZ TT Industries-built six-speed lookalike Albion gearbox, and a belt primary drive NEB clutch. The chassis package includes the legendary lightweight Egli frame, a 230mm Fontana front brake, 200mm Ceriani rear brake, Morad rims, Ceriani style

front forks with Maxton double damping, and lightweight Maxton race rear shocks.

Despite the introduction of the D Series Rapide/Black Night and Black Shadow/Black Prince in 1954, declining sales caused Vincent more and more difficulties, with production winding-up in mid-December of 1955.

The big Vincents were often referred to as the World's fastest standard motorcycles, coupled with a reputation for a 'no expense spared' quality manufacturing process, which was reflected in their price at the upper scale of the spectrum. The Vincent engine didn't need a Featherbed chassis, but the Featherbed frame needed a Vincent engine, so the Norvin was born, for those who could afford it. In 1988, *Café Racers* author Mike Clay described the Vincent hybrid aptly: "As the Triton was the café racer's Model T Ford, so the Norvin was the supercharged Bentley of the genre. Even today, a well tweaked Norvin could give nearly all modern machinery a fright. In the 1960s, on fast A roads it was invincible, though on twisty sections its weight inevitably told against it."

The Barton Norvin has a Manx Norton frame with a chromed Manx swinging arm and Norton forks. The wheels are from a TZ Yamaha Racing, with a four-leading-shoe brake at the front, and original DID rims with stainless steel spokes. The exhaust is a 2in custom, designed by Tony Cook. (Courtesy Mick Barton)

Mick's Norvin outside the London Ace Café, June 2009. (Courtesy Mick Barton)

BARTON NORVIN

Mick Barton built his first Norvin at the age of 16, as an apprentice to London Norton main dealer Gus Kuhn. He later left this dealership, as he wanted to go road racing, and would have had to work on Saturdays at Gus Kuhn's, which didn't match up. Mick also raced sidecars at all levels, and was European Champion in 1982. He further raced at Grand Prix level and was second at the Le Mans Grand Prix. Mick is now 67 years old and still riding and restoring old bikes, and intending to again parade a classic sidecar at the Spa Classics in Belgium in 2016.

His Norvin, right, is fitted with a 1000cc race engine (prepared by Chris Chant), sporting a lightened and balanced flywheel, lightened cams and steel idler, new Omega 8:1 pistons (low compression pistons installed for ease of kicking over), four-plug heads with big valves; all held in with custom-designed and made-engine plates. The clutch and belt drive are Newby items and the four-speed Quaife Wasp motorcross gearbox is stronger to cope with the torque from a Vincent engine. Also fitted to the gearbox is a KTM aluminium kickstart and custom shaft, rounded-off with a laser-cut gearbox cap. The custom-made aluminium fuel tank is based on a four-gallon Manx tank, with a Monza filler cap. The oil tank is incorporated into the rear of the custom-made seat. The engine is fed by 17/32 GP polished carburettors with TT floats, and the magneto is a Lucas racing item with stainless armature. The rear chain is DID, as supplied to 500cc Moto GP teams. A Boyer Bransden power box is fitted instead of a battery, and a small lightweight Kubota alternator runs between clutch and belt, driven from the front engine sprocket. Custom cables are made by Venhills, in silver, and the frame paintjob is an Audi pearlised orange. This stunning café racer has now been sold to an Italian collector, and Mick is well on his way to completing his next Norvin.

The Café Racer's frame has a nickel finish and is fitted with 35mm Ceriani-type forks. The bike is delivered with a 5in speedo, a 3in Smith tachometer, a stainless steel battery carrier, and solo seat rear sets. (Courtesy Paul Coene)

Banana-shaped aluminium fuel tank and Godet's special exhaust system. (Courtesy Paul Coene)

GODET CAFÉ RACER

Paul Coene is the lucky owner of the beautiful air-cooled 50-degree V-twin Egli-Vincent, left, built by Patrick Godet in France. It's Godet's café racer version without the fairing, which for Paul makes it much more comfortable than a clip-on model. Normally, Godet uses the Black Shadow specification, with a displacement of 998cc and a bore x stroke of 84x90mm, but in Paul's case, the engine is not a 998, but a 1330cc (92x100mm). His bike's 1330 engine has the same bore and stroke as the 1000cc Vincent, and therefore the same torque characteristics, which makes it such a nice, smooth power plant. But, of course, the performance is much higher. The Vincent, with its tubular steel spine frame, is fitted with a four-speed gearbox, 230mm Fontana type magnesium four-leading-shoe brakes, and a Black Lightning type rear hub. The wheelbase of the bike is 1445mm (57in) and the weight with oil amounts to 172kg (378lb).

EGLI RACING

Famous Swiss engine tuner and chassis creator Fritz W Egli Sr has already been mentioned in this chapter. His business started in a converted cow shed in Bettwil, a village situated on the highest point of the county Aargau, 3km east of Lake Hallwiler. Egli came up with his first ever central tube frame to improve the handling of his beloved Black Lightning racer in 1966, and subsequently won the Swiss Mountain Championship with his Vincent in 1968. Other racers cottoned on to using his frame kit, with equal success, and the rest is history. It's a design which, basically, stood the test of time in road and racing use until the present day. Between 1968 and 1972, he built around 200 Egli Vincents, but his frames were also used for many other engines, like Honda or Kawasaki inline four-cylinder motors, even BMW's 'flying brick' received the Egli treatment. To the surprise of many, the 2014 Classic TT was the first visit to the Isle of Man for the retired 77 year old frame builder.

The Egli Triumph shown bottom-right was built by a gent near Bournemouth, using a Malem frame and a Bonneville spec engine.

He used Roadholder forks with Triumph conical hubs front and rear, altered to look like Manx Norton hubs. The front brake plate is also Triumph, but slightly earlier, from the late '60s, machined to fit. The Egli chassis was so popular that numerous UK workshops started to make their own replicas, aided by the absence of a registered trademark by Fritz Egli, and a UK regulation that allowed prototype registrations. Cyril Malem's firm, CTG Developments, in Wimborne, Dorset was one such company.

The next Triumph was built by Fritz Egli as a red-painted Egli-Triumph T120 in 1971, and bought by a French enthusiast, and quite possibly the only one of its kind in France back then. An engine blowup in 1974 and the subsequent sale of the frame to a Vincent enthusiast, put a halt to the bike's history. It wasn't until the mid-'90s that the resurrection of the Egli-Triumph began, but, this time, with a frame reproduced by

Vincents on display in Godet's showroom. (Courtesy Patrick Godet)

Some original Egli frames on display in the firm's little upstairs museum in Bettwil.

Egli Triumph 650 – a rare sight. (Courtesy www.ventureclassics.co.uk)

The T120 engine is fitted with a 750cc Morgo kit, and features 34mm Mikuni carburettors, a balanced crankshaft, and a T140 five-speed gearbox, plus a resurfaced and improved head by The Cylinder Head Shop, front brake by Ceriani, and Triumph conical rear hub. (Courtesy Cedric Janodet)

Above right: Egli Senior and Egli Junior in unison. (Courtesy F Egli). The prototype, above, is powered by a Godet-built Vincent replica engine, with a displacement of 1330cc and a bore x stroke of 90x102mm, producing 110hp @ 5600rpm. (Courtesy JM Losma/FW Egli Jnr)

CTG again. It helped said UK firm that the owner kept the original '70s parts from the frame that connected the cylinder head to the top beam.

Fritz W Egli Junior went his own way, working for development departments for Formula 1 firms, lastly with Suter Racing Technology, while also always having a passion for motorcycles (especially Ducatis), through early exposure to bikes in his father's workshop. A 2012 visit to former Egli employee Terry Prince, in Australia, led to Terry hatching the idea of creating a contemporary interpretation of the classic Vincent backbone frame. With himself taking care of the marketing side of the venture, Egli would be tasked with the implementation of the project. Since then, Egli Junior undertook some CAD design, and engaged his former employer Suter to produce the new concept modelled by Egli, along with some other components. The Vincent-

Öhlins FGRT/S46 forks with 25-degree rake and 103mm trail, Suter-Egli 2-in-1 exhaust with Akrapovic silencer, electronic ignition, five-speed gear box, 1430mm wheelbase, CNC-milled alloy spine frame with integrated oil tank (weight 6.5kg), solid-milled alloy rear swingarm with directly operated Öhlins monoshock, PVM alloy wheels, and a wet weight of 166kg (Courtesy JM Losma/FW Egli Jnr)

powered prototype was unveiled in racing shape in 2015, initially with Ducati fuel tank and bodywork for track testing, almost 50 years after Egli Senior released his original frame kit. Suter Racing designer David Roth is tasked to model a road and racing version of the bike for a small production run, and frame kits for existing Vincent owners are also planned, further down the track. It's nice to see the Egli lineage continuing successfully.

WESLAKE

Harry Weslake is one of Exeter's favourite sons. Born in August 1897, his first foray into two wheels was at the tender age of 15 on a Swiss Motosacoche, where the speed of his mount acquainted him quickly with the local police force. At 16, he set about modifying a Rudge Multi for competition use in local Exeter hill climbs, thus soon expanding his reputation as a fast rider – helped also by having been in an off the cuff race with 1913 Senior TT competitor Reg Holloway. Harry developed, and was later granted the patent of, the Wex carburettor in 1918 (a name created from the names Weslake and Exeter). The carburettor soon attracted the attention of the racing fraternity and led him to a contract to work on Sunbeam competition engines. Talent breeds opportunity, hence Weslake was approached by WO Bentley to tune its racing car cylinder heads, which resulted in Bentley winning the first four places at Le Mans in 1929. In the '30s, Harry went on to design cylinder heads for firms such as Austin (notably the Mini model), SS Cars (the predecessor for Jaguar), and MG. After the war, Weslake set up a research center in Rye, Sussex. In the late '40s, Norton also hired Weslake to improve the gas flow of its Manx engine. After the inception of the Vanwall F1 team, Harry was hired to improve the venture's Ferrari cylinder heads. He was also involved in the making of every Jaguar engine, right through to the early '70s, and was commissioned by Rickman to develop an eight-valve cylinder head conversion for the Triumph 650cc twins (the basis of the TSS eight-valve Triumph model), which Dave Nourish improved upon after Weslake's demise. In 1974, the company developed a speedway engine to compete against the established Jawa power plant, leading to Peter Collins winning the 1976 World Speedway Championship in Poland, with a Weslake engine. In September 1978, engineering genius Harry Weslake passed away aged 81 while attending the World Speedway Championship in Wembley. In the '80s, the company produced a 998cc OHC ten-valve V-twin, similar to an earlier eight-valve engine.

Lastly, Lord Hesketh had commissioned Weslake to develop a 992cc air-cooled 90-degree V-twin for its Hesketh V1000, in 1977 – a bike which went into production in 1981.

A 120hp Weslake 998cc V-twin speedway sidecar, built in 1980 by Graeme Hewitson, and first raced in the 1985-86 season. The outfit is part of the E Hayes Motorworks Collection in Invercargill, NZ, the home of Burt Munro's 'The World's Fastest Indian.'

The Weslake Vendetta, as tested in September 1975. The ancestor of the 500cc motor produced 58hp @ 9500rpm, with a compression ratio of 11:1: good for a 125mph top speed. (Courtesy Motorcycle Sport)

Bill rode this 350cc Manx on the road, and raced it; seen here parked in Turvey, Ireland, 1975. (Courtesy Bill Anderson)

WESLAKE VENDETTA

In the '70s, Welsh policeman John Caffrey begged Weslake to provide him with a 500cc eight-valve engine variant of its 750cc power plant, for his club racer aspirations. Weslake obliged, and the first 500cc engine for a private user was fitted into a Manx frame, to take part in the 1972 Manx Senior GP. For the 1973 Manx GP, Caffrey teamed up with Stan Cooke (maker of Avon fairing fittings in Wales) to build their own so-called Vendetta frame. Cooke later produced more versions of this frame, using predominantly G50 engines.

CALIFORNIAN WESLAKE-NORTON

Bill Anderson from California also owns a Weslake-powered Norton, a bike he's owned since 1967. It started life as a Model 50, and over the years has had a number of power plants, notably a 650 Triumph, a 350 Manx, a 500T, and two Weslake engines. Bill was living in Ireland when he fitted the Weslake motor. The idea was to see how a Weslake would do as a short circuit racer. When he moved home to California, he felt he was a bit old for road racing... so he went land speed racing instead. The Weslake Norton currently holds the 500cc APS/PG (A=special construction, PS=partial streamlining, PG=pushrod gas) record at 129.915mph, set at El Mirage dry lake in southern California. This record was set in 2007, and still stands today. The bike hasn't run for a few years now, as a Weslake single sidecar racer has occupied his time since then. Bill's Weslake Norton is an early Weslake, usually referred to as a long-rod engine. The Weslake in his sidecar is a later short-rod engine.

Bill points out that the Weslake Norton doesn't look as good as it does with a Manx motor, but the Weslake is a faster engine. (Courtesy Bill Anderson)

Kiwi – Weston

Cloud Craig-Smith: "Peter Haugh bought this bike as a standard Norton Dominator, with its Weslake speedway motor fitted, in the '90s, as a complete but unfinished project. He then painted it blue and asked me to race it. It has since become a surprisingly fast machine, after a lot of hard work and constant development over the years spent on it. Some main improvements have been a Grimeca front brake, a complete McIntosh racing Manx Norton frame, Alloy tank, TT Industries gearbox and, lately, some engine tuning by Eric Swinbourne. I rode the Weston in the early development years and won the New Zealand Classic Motorcycle Racing Register (NZCMRR) Championship in the up-to 600cc pre-75 Post Classic class in 1998 on it. Mike McMurtry took over riding the bike through the early 2000s, and Eric now rides the bike in some NZ South Island events."

Peter Haugh's 1971 500cc Weslake Norton Special. The Weston racer is shown in the pit lane at NZ's Burt Munro Challenge Invercargill Street Race, November 2015, ridden by Cloud Craig Smith.

113

WESLAKE – RUDGE 500E

In January 1981 *Motorcycle News* reported on the first public appearance of a new Rudge motorcycle in 40 years, in the form of a Weslake speedway engined Rudge, with the designation 500E. The bike made its debut at the Racing & Sporting Show in London in road race trim, after successful track tests for almost a year had encouraged Ron Gardner, one of the men at the heart of the project, to gauge the interest of potential customers at the show.

The Weslake engine was still shown in speedway form, with its total loss oil system, hence the large aluminium catch tank underneath the frame. The monoshock frame had the engine hanging from the top spine, giving it strength and light weight simultaneously. Weslake were working on the oil being carried in the spine tube, above the engine, for a conversion to a dry sump system, but sadly a road version of this Rudge prototype for lovers of the big British single wasn't meant to be.

The Rudge 500E featured a Tony Foale cantilever frame and Foale wheels, based on the John Player Nortons. The Weslake DOHC four-valve single-cylinder engine produced 60hp, was fitted with a Quaife gearbox, and had a weight of 300lb (136kg). (Courtesy Tony Foale)

TROCKEL WESLAKE RACERS

During his student years, Jochen Trockel worked in a BSA workshop run by Hein Gericke, in Duesseldorf. Needless to say, his ride became a BSA Rocket 3 750cc, a bike he's owned since 1973. The 1969 Rocket 750 didn't fit the German racing regulations, so, in 1993 he started with classic racing on a Triumph, and from 1999 onwards, on a Weslake 500. Jochen finds the mechanical side of the Rocket 3, Triumph, and Weslake bikes very similar, along with their special tools and general know-how about them. But above all, he's a good friend of now 84 year old Dave Nourish, who still helps riders wherever he can. He was also the engineer responsible for Jochen's engines at the Weslake works, before he went into retirement. Jochen raced against Dave Nourish, and also John Loder (RIP), who rode Dave's works Weslake, both always much faster than him. In 2000, Jochen was second fastest newcomer, in 30th place out of 100 competitors. If everything went well, which was seldom, he achieved the midfield position of 30-35 from 70-100 starters, with usually only 45-50 riders crossing the finishing line. His tally amounted to four finisher's medals, with his brother gaining two. As a privateer on the IoM, Jochen always had to repair, fund, and ride the machines all by himself. This often meant only two to three hours' sleep at night, due to overnight repairs to ready the bikes for the next day. All this would have been impossible without help from friends and girlfriends, in order to manage two practice rounds per day during training week, and four rounds of 62km on the mountain course on race day.

RICKMAN / WESLAKE 500

This rare enough and original 1968 Weslake bike was Jochen's ride on the IoM from 2000-2003, and he also used it for a demo lap at the 2015 Festival of Jurby Classic event. Wheels and frame/swinging arm

The original 360-degree parallel-twin has its camshaft, etc, in bronze bearings, and produces approx 51hp @ 8500rpm, with an 11.5-12:1 compression ratio. Note pre-ride checklist written in German on the fuel tank.

Closeup of the Weslake 500 engine and carburettor.

are by Rickman, with Lockheed disc brakes. The original super light and stiff Rickman racing front fork tube diameter is 41mm, with only 1,2mm thickness! It's a much more forgiving, and less vulnerable ride than his other bike, shown next – but not as fast either. The transmission is an original Quaife five-speed on a Norton base.

SEELEY MK 3/WESLAKE 500

Jochen rode this Seeley MK 3/Weslake 500 from 2004 to 2008 on the IoM. This bike is essentially a replica, with a red painted open Seeley MK 3 frame of Reynolds tubing, weighing a mere 8.5kg. The front is fitted with a magnesium CMA four-shoe brake, with a 262mm diameter disc, and the front fork consists of a Seeley replica from Dick Hunt, made from magnesium. The 500cc engine's 90-degree crankshaft, camshafts, and roller tappets are all on needle bearings. The six-speed Quaife magnesium transmission is also on needle bearings, and the rear wheel is again a Dick Hunt Seeley replica, with a magnesium drum.

WESLAKE 900CC SPECIAL

The Norton Manx-Weslake special below was sold by Bonhams for £11,500. This beauty started life as a dismantled 1951 Norton ES2, which, in 1994, received a '50s Manx Featherbed frame upgrade, sourced from racer Dan Shorey, and the addition of a wide swinging arm and Roadholder forks. Next, a new 180-degree crankshaft NRE Weslake engine joined the club, with a longer driveside mainshaft to accommodate the alternator, all specially built by Dave Nourish. The motor was initially fitted with a Bob Newby 30mm belt primary drive and clutch, driving an AMC gearbox fitted with a Quaife five-speed cluster, an Interspan ignition, and 36mm Amal carburettors. This was followed by an alloy fuel and oil tank, alloy wheel rims and mudguards, a CMA 8LS front brake, Triumph conical hub rear brake, and a stainless steel racing dimension exhaust. Later, the motor was refreshed by Dave Nourish again, and the headstock of the frame fitted with a strengthening brace, alongside a wide oval section

Power output is 56hp @ 9500rpm, with a compression ratio of 13:1 – pretty quick, but susceptible to damage. (Courtesy Jochen Trockel)

swinging arm with taper roller bearings. The gearbox outer covers were also altered, to accept a kickstart and Manx clutch release mechanism. Lastly, a 40mm primary drive and narrow alternator, a modified instrument cluster, and a Manx fly screen completed the package.

The Weslake 900 café racer is fitted with a Fontana magnesium alloy four-leading-shoe front brake, Maxton suspension front and rear, Yamaha TD rear wheel, large capacity oil tank, with extra clearance for the 36mm Mikuni flat slide carburettors, and has a mere wet weight of 356.4lb (162kg). (Courtesy Bonhams)

CHAPTER 7
CAFÉ RACER RESOURCES

Ace Café

The Ace Café, on London's North Circular Road, started life in 1938 as a 24-hour transport café for truck drivers, but soon developed into a popular meeting place for motorcyclists. A World War Two air raid destroyed the venue, requiring a rebuild in 1949. The Ton-Up Boys, and later the Rockers, arrived on the scene with their bikes in the evening for a dose of rock 'n' roll music and socialising, before engaging in burn-ups after midnight, when traffic was low on the North Circular route.

The Ace café attracted its fair share of followers, and also opponents, over the years, due to the rate of speed-related accidents en-route to and from the venue – ripe fodder for the press in its day. A downturn in business caused the Ace to close its doors in 1969, when the building was sold to a tyre fitting chain. The first annual Ace Café Reunion was organised by Mark Wilsmore and friends in 1994, to mark the 25th anniversary of the café's closure, attracting thousands of visitors. Due to space constraints, the organisers soon set up the Brighton Burn-up & Ride with the Rockers run, which has been an integral part of Ace Café Reunions since 1996, held on Brighton seafront's Madeira Drive.

The Ace Café was reopened in 1997, completely refurbished by 2001, and has since once again become a favourite meeting point for Rockers and other two- and four-wheeled petrol heads – but this time from all over the world. An extensive annual calendar of events for both motorbike and car owners ensures that the Ace Café is here to stay for some time to come.

www.ace-café-london.com

Ace Café flyers for the 2015 Café Reunion and Brighton Burn-Up. (Courtesy Ace Café)

AJS

The AJS & Matchless Owners Club Ltd runs its own spares scheme, organises an International Rally in May, a UK National rally in August, and a second national back-to-basics rally in October each year. The club also distributes its monthly magazine *Jampot* to its worldwide audience

www.jampot.com

Ariel

The best point of contact for anyone interested in Ariel bikes is the Ariel Owners Motorcycle Club (AOMCC), founded at the London Ace Café in November 1951. The club holds many events annually, and has branches throughout the UK. Its monthly magazine *Cheval de Fer* informs all full members of all things Ariel related.

www.arielownersmcc.co.uk

BSA

The BSA Owners Club (BSAOC) was founded in 1958 and is the largest classic motorcycle club in the UK. Its magazine *The Star* is published on the first of every month.

www.bsaownersclub.co.uk

The BSA Gold Star Owners Club is devoted to the preservation, maintenance and enjoyment of BSA Gold Star and Rocket Gold Star motorcycles.

www.bsagoldstarownersclub.com

Busy Bee Café

The Busy Bee, on the A41, was also a transport café, open around the clock, seven days a week, where motorcyclists met to hang out, listen to music, and then ride off. The following website from the Busy Bee Motorcycle Club chronicles the history of this café:

busybeemcc.wordpress.com/history

Cafés

See **Ace Café**, **Busy Bee Café**, and **Johnsons**

The 59 Club

The 59 Club was founded in the London suburb of Hackney Wick in April 1959, by Rev John Oates, as a Church of England-based youth club. In the same year, Father Bill Shergold had been appointed vicar of St Mary at Eton, where he developed a desire to reach out to the young and disaffected bikers, which were considered antisocial by the media of their time, and therefore not welcomed in many places. In 1962, Shergold, a motorcyclist himself, summoned the courage and rode his Triumph to the Ace Café on London's North Circular Road, to invite the rockers to his Eton Mission on Saturday evenings. This was well received and prompted the birth of the motorcycle section of

MEMORIES OF THE 59 CLUB BY STEWART WILKINS

"My first encounter with Father Bill was at the vicarage, one weekend before the clubhouse had opened in Paddington Green. I rode there on my Norton, with my girlfriend on the cramped so-called 'dual racing seat.' We had a cup of tea and biscuits with Father Bill, alongside a few other motorcyclists in a very friendly and congenial atmosphere, where religion was not thrust upon you.

"The clubhouse opened in 1965, and was initially only open on a Thursday and Saturday. You had to be under twenty-five years old to join or, if older, approved by the Club leaders for a joining fee of five shillings (25p).

"There was a helmet/clothing park on the ground floor, along with refreshments – no alcohol. Upstairs was the main meeting hall where social functions were held and groups played, on some nights. The upstairs had a wooden floor, so rather than clapping, one would stamp your feet so the whole floor shook!

Cover page of the 59 Club's *Link* magazine, Vol 1 No 1. The May 1965 issue hails the 59 Club as the world's largest motorcycle club, with over 7000 members. (Courtesy Stewart Wilkins)

"In the summer there were loads of bikes turning up and they parked on the other side of the road to the club house, on the pathway leading up to St Mary's church. It often became very congested and difficult to get your bike in and out, so for convenience I often chose to park in the small side road near the clubhouse, where you often found the less desirable small capacity machines that the riders didn't want to show off. If you had a problem with your bike, there was always another member that would be able to help you with advice or spare parts. These times were, of course, before the days of the internet, and there were only the monthly motorcycle magazines to glean help and information from.

"There were organised rides to various places that you could join-in with, and it was always a great feeling riding through London with a group of motorcycles.

"I met a lot of interesting people and made many friends during those days, and it made a change from the coffee bars that were the usual hangouts. Saying that, the Ace Café (this was the original Ace, with fixed Formica tables and chairs, and the tea spoon was on a chain on the front counter) was only a short detour on the way home, so made for a longer evening if wanted."

the 59 Club. Shergold became known as Father Bill and was labelled by some 'the ton-up vicar,' holding services for the rockers, blessing their bikes, but also helping members in trouble with the authorities. In 1965, Shergold moved from Hackney Wick to Paddington St Mary's, where he continued as a vicar until 1969. He then became the vicar of St Bartholomew's in Charlton-by-Dover, where he founded the 69 Club.

The club's official website is **www.the59club.co.uk**

The Spirit of the 59 website, **the59club.com**, is an independent site, documenting the rocker movement and history of the 59 Club.

The 69 Club: **www.69motorcycleclub.co.uk/club_history.asp**

BUSY BEE MOTORCYCLE CLUB

See **Busy Bee Café**

COTTON

The Cotton Owners & Enthusiasts Club runs a website tailored to the growing number of Cotton enthusiasts. The club also publishes its quarterly *Cotton Pickins* magazine for its esteemed members.

www.cottonownersclub.com

DRESDA AUTO TRITON

Dave Degens was taught basic engineering by his father, with whom he joined to make scientific instruments at the age of 16. His first motorbike was a 350cc army Matchless 350, but he soon progressed to a BSA Gold Star 500cc. One of his friends encouraged him to go racing, and the prize money seemed good, so he raced initially on the Gold Star, later buying an AJS 350 7R to be more competitive.

After being drafted for National Service, he was asked to compete in the Welsh Two Day Trial for the army on a BSA 500, where

Dresda Triton 650 pre-unit. (Courtesy www.ventureclassics.co.uk)

he promptly won the army award at the trial. During his army time he also won a 350cc Brands Hatch race on a 350cc Manx Norton. After the army, an opportunity beckoned to buy the Dresda Autos business, in Putney, with his neighbour Dick Boon, who he bought-out a few years later. Dave made good money winning races at circuits such as Brands Hatch and Mallory Park, and he also won the Thruxton 500 Mile race, in 1964, while racing for Aermacchi importer Sid Lawton. In the mid-'60s, Dave was amongst the top few riders in the UK. He also rode a BMW R69S in the Barcelona 24-hour race in 1964, but had gearbox issues and didn't finish. In 1965 he went again, with Rex Butcher on his self-built Manx Norton Triton T120, and won the race, a feat he repeated once more in 1970, with Ian Goddard as his co-rider. The Dresda Autos business was doing well when Japauto asked Dave to build a lightweight frame for its racing Hondas in France: the Honda racer went on to won the Bol d'Or two years in a row. Dresda's reputation for building racing bikes for the road subsequently grew. Dave, naturally, also continued to build Dresda Tritons, or prepare the engines and parts for customers who wanted to build their own Tritons.

Festivals
Austrian Tridays

In 2005, screenwriter and Triumph fan Uli Brée came up with the idea of staging a Triumph party bonanza in the small town of Neukirchen, near Salzburg, Austria. He got together with the local tourism board and Triumph Germany, and the rest is history. Since then, Neukirchen turns British for three days every June, and transforms into Newchurch, where up to 20,000 two-wheel enthusiasts from all over the world come together to celebrate Triumph motorcycles in all shapes or form. Anyone who thinks three days are too short to explore the stunning surroundings should consider Triweek, where you can indulge in a whole week of Triumph action and take part in guided tours to suit every visitor's needs.

www.tridays.com

Tridays poster from 2015. (Courtesy Neukirchen Tourism Board)

France

France's *Café Racer* magazine organizes its fourth Café Racer Festival weekend in 2016, at the historic 1924-built Linas-Montlhéry racing circuit, 30km south of Paris. The estimated crowd of 10,000 participants is expected to see about 300 motorcycles riding 28 demo laps around the oval shaped track, grouped into vintage and modern café racers, race bikes, and an all-female class. A sprint tournament will see amateurs and professionals pitch themselves in playoff duels on a 200 metre standing start track. An exhibitor's village will host all major bike manufacturers' new model line-ups, along with stands of popular names from the custom bike scene, while several competitions will reward the best prepared café racers in attendance. Triumph's Street Twin Project dealer competition, for the best interpretation of its newly released Street Twin, will be unveiling its favourites as a preview to the festival, and will also participate in the sprint event. Evening concerts, an art installation, and the screening of popular motorcycle movies will round off the festival programme.

www.café-racer.fr

Germany – Glemseck 101

The Glemseck 101 is the largest outdoors motorcycle event in Germany. Since its inception in 2005, it has evolved to reach over 75,000 visitors as one of the largest motorcycle gatherings in Europe, and celebrated its tenth anniversary in 2015. Bike aficionados usually gather on the first weekend in September at Hotel Glemseck, on the former Solitude race track in Leonberg, near Stuttgart. It has become the premier meeting place for international bike customisers and been described by many as Europe's best melting pot for lovers of the café racer culture. The event consists of ride-outs, a dealer mile, live music, bike presentations, a stage programme, and, since 2009, has held ⅛ mile sprints on the home stretch of the Solitude track, made even more popular with the 2011 introduction of the International Café Racer Sprint class, for bike industry professionals.

The former 22.3km Solitude mountain course racetrack (named after a castle in the area) dates to 1903, initially only for motorcycle competitions, but later for car racing too. Between 1935 and 1937, the track was shortened to 11.5km, with its start and finishing line at the Glemseck Lake House. After the war, racing resumed in 1949, with the first race attracting 300,000 spectators. In 1951, FIM granted Germany the right to hold world championship

Glemseck Poster from 2013. (Courtesy Steven Flier)

events again from the following year, and 1954 an estimated 435,000 visitors came to watch the likes of Werner Haas on a 250cc NSU, Geoff Duke on a 500cc Gilera, or the popular sidecar class, with team Noll/Cron winning their respective race categories. Other big names, such as Bill Lomas and Carlo Ubbiali in 1956, and Gary Hocking and John Surtees in 1960, graced the historic race track with their presence. 1964 marked the last motorcycle Grand Prix on the Solitude, with riders such as Jim Redman, Phil Read, and Mike Hailwood bringing home the bacon.

www.glemseck101.de

**Glemseck Party Poster 2015.
(Courtesy Florence Shirazi)**

Isle of Man – Festival of Jurby

A visit to the Isle of Man is always impressive and can be warmly recommended to any motorcyclist. The 2015 Festival of Motorcycling, which included the Classic TT and the Manx GP, made no exception. One of the many sources of eye candy during this time was the Festival of Jurby event, on 30th August, where at least 1000 classic motorcycles were to be seen and heard, with many café racers amongst them.

The village of Jurby is located in a largely agricultural district on the North-West coast of the island, and houses, amongst other things, an industrial park next to the old RAF airfield. This airfield originally served as a Royal Air Force training station during World War Two. The old runways now form the Jurby motorcycle race track, which provided the venue for a series of parade laps for classic motorcycles, with some star riders, to the delight of the estimated 12,000 or so visitors in attendance. In short, it's an event not to be missed.

New Zealand

Café racer gatherings are now a global phenomenon, and have truly spread around the world. They don't always have to be large scale events, but can be equally entertaining on a smaller level. James Chambers and Michael Dobson chose Paraparaumu on the Kapiti Coast to stage their free entry Polished Rockers Ride-in Bike Show, for custom, classic & café racer bikes, a mere 45 minute drive from the author's residence,

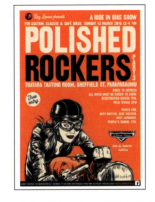

Polished Rockers NZ 2016.

New Zealand's capital city of Wellington. Prizes were awarded for Best of British (any British custom, classic or café), Best European Bike (including Scandinavian and Eastern Block bikes), Best Japanese and American bikes, Best Café Racer (low handlebars, rear set foot pegs, performance modifications, and café racer attitude), amongst other awards. Live Rockabilly music by the X-Ray Catz provided the backdrop for viewing some of the best bikes from around NZ's lower North Island region.

GREEVES

The Greeves Riders Association (GRA) is the place to go for anyone interested in Greeves hardware. The club has an annual calendar of upcoming events, and regularly publishes articles in its *Leading Link* magazine.

www.greeves-riders.org.uk

JAP

Cameron Engineering and Motorsports Ltd, UK, is concerned with the restoration and recreation of JAP type engines

cameronracingengines.com

Greg Summerton Engineering, Australia, is a JAP racing and sports engine specialist

www.eurospares.com/greg.html

JOHNSONS CAFÉ

Johnsons Café, located on the A20, close to the Brands Hatch racing circuit, near West Kingsdown, was yet another favourite hangout for UK motorcyclists in the '60s. The following website is dedicated to its history:

www.gfsmith.net/johnsons.html

MATCHLESS

See **AJS**

NORTON

The Norton Owners Club was founded in 1959 and is the organisation to join for any Norton enthusiast, be it in the search for technical advice, its spares scheme, machine dating, or library access.

www.nortonownersclub.org

NORVIN

See **Vincent**

NOURISH

Dave Nourish, of Nourish Race Engines, spent over 40 years of continued development on the original eight-valve Weslake engine.

In 2014, after Dave's well-deserved retirement, Nourish Engineering, now under Chris Bushell and based in Chiddingstone Hoath, Kent, was formed to continue Dave's legacy and to take the business further. Nourish's compact low-weight four valve per-cylinder twin power unit is coupled with a completely new and immensely strong crankcase/crankshaft assembly. This racing engine is adaptable to meet a wide range of requirements, be it from road-racing to grass-track or moto-cross competition use, in solo or sidecar guise, using petrol or dope fuels.

The package fits into any 500cc, 750cc, or 850cc motorcycle racing category, but can also be supplied with alternator crankshafts for street use. Its eight-valve conversion kit for 650cc or 750cc Triumph engines (unit or pre-unit) gives an increase in bore size to 76mm and a capacity of 749cc. Nourish also sells billet crankshafts for Triumph, Norton, and BSA twins, including a few for the Matchless G50.

www.nourishengineering.co.uk

Record racing

A term for dropping a coin into the slot of a transport café jukebox and racing to a given point and back before the record finished.

Royal Enfield

The Royal Enfield Owners Club is a forum covering the maintenance, restoration, and use of Royal Enfield motorcycles and other RE machinery. Its club magazine, *The Gun,* is published bimonthly.

www.royalenfield.org.uk

Hitchcocks Motorcycles have been dealing with UK- or Indian-built Royal Enfield's since 1984, and stock probably the worlds largest range of spares and accessories for this marque, be it for retail or motorcycle trade.

www.hitchcocksmotorcycles.com

In 2001, Royal Enfield Books publisher Gordon May created *The Bullet-In* (*TBI*) magazine, which the author fondly remembers reading when he owned a 350cc RE Bullet in New Zealand. This small, but well liked publication quickly became the magazine for all Royal Enfield Bullet enthusiasts. Gordon then went on produce quite a number of Royal Enfield motorcycle books, ranging from Redditch to Madras-built bikes.

www.royalenfieldbooks.com

Rudge

The Rudge Enthusiasts Club was founded in February 1956, in London. It's magazine, *The Radial,* has been published continuously to the present day. When the manufacture of Rudge parts came to an end in the '60s, the Club purchased the remaining Rudge spares for the benefit of its members. The club holds many factory drawings in its library, and its website operates a forum to support Rudge enthusiasts in keeping their bikes on the road.

www.rudge.co.uk

Tinker

Scotsman Jack Lennie, an individual currently working for Warner Brothers Films, designing vehicles, created Tinker, a free, downloadable, no-weld motorcycle kit, designed to rejuvenate damaged or no longer roadworthy motorcycles by re-framing their existing or purchased engine and running gear, all of this conceived over a 32-week period during his product design studies at Edinburgh Napier University. His CAD/CAM kit has been designed to accommodate almost every type of motorcycle engine and can handle speeds of up to 225km/h (140mph). For peace of mind, Tinker also complies with UK and European Union transport vehicle standards to ensure user safety.

The Tinker prototype shown has a GPZ 500 engine test-fitted to it. (Courtesy Jack Lennie)

Once the open source distribution is sorted, simply download the kit and take it to your local CAD/CAM software equipped engineering workshop, have the parts cut, and take them home for assembly, with no specialist tools required.

For more info, see **www.jacklenniedesigner.com**

Ton Up Boys (Rockers)

A name derived from 'doing a ton,' an informal English term for riding at a speed of 100mph (160km/h), a popular sport of the café racer movement in the '50s and '60s.

Triton

The Triton Owners Club of Great Britain was formed by Steve Blackwell and Cliff Groom in 2000, as a medium to exchange tips and tricks with fellow Triton owners. It's quarterly club newsletter contains re-build stories, technical notes, club merchandise, and a free advertising platform for its members.

www.triton-owners-club.co.uk

TRIUMPH

The Triumph Owners' Motorcycle Club (TOMCC) was formed in 1949 by a group of dedicated Triumph buffs in South London. The club now caters for all Triumph enthusiasts, be they concerned with pre-Meriden bikes up to 1942, the Meriden Classic Er a, or the modern Hinckley Triumph range.

www.tomcc.org

The Riders Association of Triumph (RAT) is a motorcycle club for Hinckley-built Triumph's

www.triumphmotorcycles.co.uk/inside-triumph/rat

The Triumph Rat Net is an online forum for all things Triumph

www.triumphrat.net

Bonnefication. This website was founded in 2008 and is an online magazine dedicated to modified Hinckley Triumph Twins

www.bonnefication.com

VELOCETTE

The Velocette Owners Club has 2500 members worldwide, and is concerned with the marque's single-cylinder Velocette models. The club set up Veloce Spares Ltd to help its members to keep its bikes on the road. The Owners Club journal *Fishtail* is published eight times per annum.

www.velocetteowners.com

VILLIERS

Villiers Services, based in the West Midlands, are the world's largest stockist of Villiers spares. The company also deals with Greeves, James, Francis Barnett, DMW, and Cotton spares.

villiersservices.co.uk

VINCENT

The Vincent HRD Owners Club was founded in 1948 and has continued to flourish ever since, with almost 2500 worldwide members today. In the UK, a rally is held annually, with an international rally held every four years. The club's journal, *mph*, is published monthly and is a great read for all Vincent topics.

www.voc.uk.com.

The website **www.vincentownersclub.co.uk** has a forum section for Norvin owners, as does **www.thevincent.com/NorvinTechSection.html**

WESLAKE

See **Nourish** entry

Z

Ze end ☺

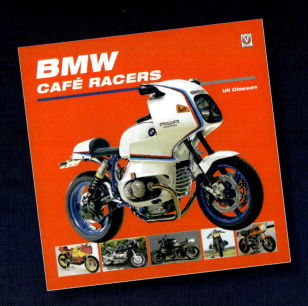

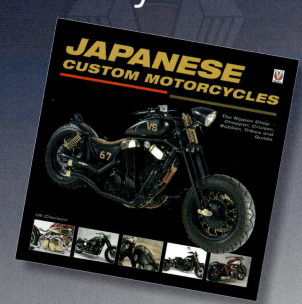

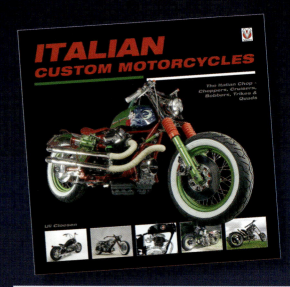

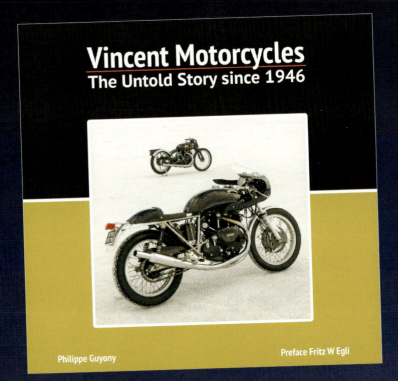

Index